A Moving
Meditation

OTHER BOOKS FROM BRIGHT LEAF

A Moving Meditation

*Life on a Cape Cod
Kettle Pond*

Stephen G. Waller

BRIGHT LEAF
BOOKS THAT ILLUMINATE
Amherst and Boston
An imprint of University of Massachusetts Press

A Moving Meditation has been supported by the Regional Books Fund, established by donors in 2019 to support the University of Massachusetts Press's Bright Leaf imprint.

Bright Leaf, an imprint of the University of Massachusetts Press, publishes accessible and entertaining books about New England. Highlighting the history, culture, diversity, and environment of the region, Bright Leaf offers readers the tools and inspiration to explore its landmarks and traditions, famous personalities, and distinctive flora and fauna.

ISBN 978-1-62534-774-9 (paper); 775-6 (hardcover)

Designed by Sally Nichols
Set in Minion Pro and Benton Modern Display
Printed and bound by Books International, Inc.

Cover design by Sally Nichols
Cover art by Coni Porter, *Long Pond on Cape Cod,* 2023.

Library of Congress Cataloging-in-Publication Data
Names: Waller, Stephen G. 1951– author.
Title: A moving meditation : life on a Cape Cod kettle pond / Stephen Glenn Waller.
Other titles: Life on a Cape Cod kettle pond
Description: Amherst : Bright Leaf, an imprint of University of Massachusetts Press [2023] | Includes bibliographical references.
Identifiers: LCCN 2023013581 (print) | LCCN 2023013582 (ebook) | ISBN 9781625347749 (paperback) | ISBN 9781625347756 (hardcover) | ISBN 9781685750473 (ebook) | ISBN 9781685750480 (ebook)
Subjects: LCSH: Long Pond (Barnstable County, Mass.)—History. | Waller, Stephen G. 1951—Homes and haunts. | Natural history—Massachusetts—Long Pond (Barnstable County)
Classification: LCC F72.C3 W35 2023 (print) | LCC F72.C3 (ebook) | DDC 974.4/92—dc23/eng/20230606
LC record available at https://lccn.loc.gov/2023013581
LC ebook record available at https://lccn.loc.gov/2023013582

British Library Cataloguing-in-Publication Data
A catalog record for this book is available from the British Library.

*To Jane, my lifelong partner and fellow
herring enthusiast*

Contents

Preface

Unobtrusive on a shelf in my crowded library during the snowy days of February was Sigurd Olsen's wonderful 1982 book *Of Time and Place*.[1] The winter had dragged darkly on, and the pandemic hung ominously over every human event. Ice and cold air temperatures kept me from my usual daily canoe excursions on the fifty-acre lake out our back door on Cape Cod. As I reread Olson's series of poignant essays about canoes, campsites, wilderness, predators, and humankind, they resonated deeply with my own recent experiences on a Cape Cod kettle pond.

I share Olsen's profound reverence for the Boundary Waters wilderness and the big lakes along the Canada-Minnesota border. He spent most of his twentieth-century life living on Burntside Lake, west of Ely. He refers to his canoe trip partners as "voyageurs"; in return, they called him "Bourgeoise," a title of respect given by the original voyageurs to their leaders. Fifty years ago, I paddled and portaged those original voyageurs' routes and magical lakes in the Hudson's Bay watershed on both sides of the international border with my Boy Scout troop, including my younger brother and my dad, an adult leader.

Both Dad and Jeff are gone now. They would agree that we struggled during those two weeks with fierce headwinds, feisty northern pike, and finding the best campsite, but with few of the tedious details of civilized life. The rich memories of those transcendent weeks are revived in a delightful way by Olson's eloquent words.

Henry David Thoreau further inspired me with his writing about Walden Pond, a kettle pond ninety miles north of the similar kettle pond I share with my Centerville, Cape Cod, neighbors. Thoreau famously wrote, "I went to the woods because I wished to live deliberately, to front only the essential facts of life, and see if I could not learn what it had to teach, and not, when I came to die, discover that I had not lived."[2]

Thoreau writes of lying back in his canoe on Walden Pond, letting the paddle rest, and allowing the canoe to drift wherever the wind and current took him until he bumped against the shore, driven there by the breeze during his long reverie. *"Sometimes as I drift idly on Walden Pond, I cease to live and begin to be."* On this point, I don't agree with Thoreau. I am most alive and in the moment when paddling, reacting to the wind, waves, and nearby wildlife. The canoe is an ideal device for moving meditation. Thoreau's kettle pond is very similar to mine, but I believe that mine is best experienced moving actively, not passively.

My family and I were fortunate to live along the Sudbury River in Thoreau's Concord for several years during our medical training. On several warm summer days, we swam together across the iconic Walden Pond. I hoped then to someday live on a kettle pond, as deliberately and thoughtfully as Thoreau did nearly two centuries earlier.

As an answer to that dream, I now live on the shore of an enchanting kettle pond on Cape Cod, one of seven on the Cape with the name Long Pond. It is a gem, too precious to carry such a redundant name. Thoreau noted there were so many "herring rivers" on the Cape that they might be more numerous than the fish! He wrote little about the kettle ponds, although they are similar to his beloved Walden. My lake is in the traditional homeland of the Mashpee Wampanoag tribe. I wish the name for our pond from the Wôpanâak language of the original Cape Cod inhabitants was known and used.

Fifty acres of cozy, intimate water that sustains a luxuriant variety of wildlife and reflects the deep blue of a clear sky. Big enough for a canoeist to feel solitude and serenity, and a full hour's paddle to make a complete lap along the shore. Small enough to not appear on large-scale maps. Big enough for a year-round coterie of geese, ducks, herons, and seasonal osprey, raising their young, squawking at each other, and entertaining us. Small enough to afford locations to spot a muskrat pup or large snapping turtle. Long Pond Centerville's intriguing history, fascinating geology, and diverse wildlife astonish me and add joy to my efforts as an amateur naturalist to understand its ecology. The inspiration that Olsen and Thoreau shared with me drives my deep affection for the pond's charming natural features. That affection is charged by the insights of Aldo Leopold, the ingenious ecologist from Wisconsin whose writings nurtured the earliest stirrings of an environmental movement in the United States. He wrote eloquently about "the oldest task in human history, to live on a piece of land without spoiling it."[3] I find that task to be a never-ending challenge at Long Pond.

Another author from my library who inspires my lake experiences is Chris Norwent, who wrote *The North of Our Lives* and *Return to Warden's Grove*, both about the Canadian Arctic and its birds and rivers.[4] In 1977–78, Norwent and five companions canoed across northern Canada, from the Rockies to Hudson's Bay, stopping for the long Arctic winter at a remote cabin in "the Barrens," north of the tree line. He returned to that cabin as an academic biologist in the summers

of 1989–91 to study the migrant sparrows. He offers many profound insights into wilderness life, the biology of living things
(not just sparrows), and unique features of the Canadian Shield
ecology. While Cape Cod has few similarities with the ecologic
details of that place, the analysis of Norwent is helpful to my
observations around Long Pond and for ideas for this book.

How remarkable freshwater lakes are! Clear, life-giving
liquid flows into a low spot and distributes itself smoothly
across its terrain. Its transparency permits observation of its
fish and turtle denizens as they move, hunt, and spawn. In
the springtime, when water clarity is at its best, one can see
six meters down into it. River herring heroically swim from
the salt marsh to spawn, traveling up the narrow run that is
adjacent to our property. Pond weeds grow on its bottom,
some sending shoots and leaves to the surface. Small black
eels hide deep in the freshwater eelgrass, quillworts, and other
pond weeds. They live their adult lives in the lake and then
escape to the ocean to spawn at the end of their lives. Mussels
filter the lake water, taking microscopic nutrition, and when
they move mark its soft, sandy bottom with elegant arcs and
swiggles. Snow on the winter ice shows empty mussel shells
left by muskrats, or hippity-hop otter tracks. Stately white mute
swans cruise silently, dipping on occasion for a snack of the
lush pond weed, unceremoniously sticking their snow-white
tails straight up in the air. Coal-black cormorants stretch and
dry their wings on docks, then fly low and fast across the lake,
spooked by even remote human activity. Charismatic ospreys
and an occasional bald eagle soar high above the water, diving
savagely when a shadow or ripple indicates a vulnerable fish
near the surface, often coming up wet and empty-handed. And
wind whispers as it passes across the smooth surface of the
transparent fluid, sometimes gently, sometimes marking it with
gusts that produce corrugated patches, rolling breakers, and
even whitecaps. Along the shoreline, a tall, dense tree cover

creates a green, brown, and gray color scheme that contrasts with the seasonal blossoms of purple loosestrife, buttonbush, and cattails; the brilliant reds of the cardinals and autumn red maple leaves; and the vibrant yellows of the many orioles and goldfinches. I find myself immersed in the moment, deep in meditation, as I paddle with silent awe and observe this magical place. As Rachel Carson wisely wrote, all these things inspire a sense of wonder.

Writing this series of essays has been a mission to recover the Boundary Waters delights I share with Mr. Olsen, the vivid kettle pond delights that I share with Mr. Thoreau, and the bird fascination I share with Professor Norwent. My Cape Cod venue is as seducing and challenging as they found theirs. Like Thoreau, Charles Darwin, and John Muir, I take most of the content of my writing from my journal entries. Muir aptly wrote, "In the gardens and forests of this wonderful moraine one might spend a whole joyful life."[5] He was exactly right.

I am grateful for the wisdom and insights of my editor, Brian Halley, with this work. And I've added a haiku poem to begin each chapter, in hopes of adding a spark of joy to your reading adventure.

> *a life on Long Pond*
> *what if I passed into heaven*
> *I might not know it*

A Moving
Meditation

1

Geology

Created in a Single Moment

~

low fast-moving clouds
reflected in the placid pond
genuine delight

About eighteen thousand years ago, the northern third of
the earth was hidden beneath a mile-thick sheet of glacial
ice. Over much of the previous two million years, Northern
Hemisphere icepacks received more snow each winter than
could be melted in the following summer's heat, so the ice
got thicker and heavier. The weight of the ice crushed the soil
and stone beneath it, and inexorably pushed the leading edge
of the ice south. When the climate warmed, the ice would
retreat, in cycles of many thousands of years. This cycle of ice
ages followed by warming periods may have repeated twenty
times. During the most recent ice incursion, the leading edge
of the thick ice pushed across the Gulf of Maine and Cape
Cod Bay. It crept inexorably onward at the speed that human
fingernails grow, creating an enormous pile of rocks and sand
at its leading edge—a moraine now called Cape Cod. Long
Island in New York state was pushed up at the same time.

When the earliest Native American immigrants arrived,
a mile-high monolith of sheer ice may have dominated the
northern horizon of Cape Cod. With so much water tied up

in glacial ice, the sea level was four hundred feet lower than it is today. The islands of Nantucket and Martha's Vineyard, the remainder moraines of an earlier ice sheet migration, were contiguous with the mainland, as was an area that today is Georges Bank, prime fishing ground one hundred miles east of the Cape. As the first humans were moving into the Cape Cod and islands region, some likely walked to the present-day islands without getting their feet wet.

Glaciers have covered Cape Cod at least four times, including several eons during which they covered the entire planet, a "Snowball Earth." After the most recent glaciation, the climate slowly warmed and the ice melted. Magnificent high waterfalls poured off the high glacial wall, exceeding by many times the height and flow of modern-day Yosemite Falls. A city-sized chunk of ice (called a "serac" by geologists) fell, breaking into three pieces and creating the three distinct "kettle" depressions for a future lake. We can hope none of those early Indians was staring up at the high waterfalls when these spectacular serac drops occurred. Such events happened often on the Cape Cod moraine. Many of the Cape's thousand lakes are considered glacial kettles, created by seracs with a round lobe shape that reminded early settlers of a tea kettle.

Nearly one thousand times, the impact of a massive icefall depressed the moraine sand and rocks that had been pushed up on Cape Cod. Sandy and rocky debris in the outwash from the face of the melting glacier surrounded the three big fallen blocks of ice. The three colossal ice blocks lay near enough to each other that they slowly melted into a single three-lobed lake. The lake, created in an instant by chunks of ice, took on its own ecology. It drained a small surrounding watershed, but there was no stream or river to bring in new water, and no surface route for its water to escape, even during wet times. Instead, its water level was controlled entirely by the Cape's immense underground freshwater aquifer, which flows slowly eastward. It fills the three lobes of Long Pond from below and then accepts water back from it, keeping the lake's level well above modern sea levels.

The immense front wall of melting glacial ice withdrew back toward the north, and other huge ice blocks crashed off, creating the larger Lake Wequaquet, only a quarter mile north of the three-lobed lake. As the glacier melted further and disappeared into Cape Cod Bay and the Gulf of Maine, the present-day Cape and its nearby islands became patches of earth surrounded by the rising sea. Much of the bare land left by the retreating glacier would be called tundra today. Sea level reached its present-day level about six thousand years ago. Some kettle ponds were drowned by the rising sea. Salt Pond at the Cape Cod National Seashore Visitor Center changed from freshwater kettle to a salt marsh. From space, the Cape Cod moraine today looks much like an arm extending from the southeast coast of Massachusetts, elbow bent at Chatham, fingers curled back at Provincetown. The resemblance is striking.

Most geologic processes take eons to complete—time way beyond our ability to comprehend. That time extends back 4.5 billion years, to the earliest cluster of space rocks called Earth. Humans think in terms of years or lifetimes, not eons. We know the words, but the concepts do not compute in our minds. In geological terms, being above sea level is a temporary condition. The oldest living things are a few thousand years old. For us and several of the large animals and trees, we may have a century at most to grow, learn, reproduce, and die. For smaller animals, a few or a dozen years is all they have. For insects and many plants, it may be one season or even just a few weeks. All those time scales are vanishingly small on the geologic scale, which marks its activity in the millions of years.

A stone casually tossed from the shoreline into Long Pond may sink and settle to the bottom. Sediment gradually covers it. In a future ice age, the stone may be scraped up and pushed south by glacial activity. It could be ground down into sand by earthquakes or eroded into the ocean. It may ride along intact with the tectonic plate crust until subsumed into the earth's mantle, there to be melted into individual liquid molecules. It may still be around as a stone when our dying sun explodes into a giant nuclear ball of fire and engulfs the earth several billion years from now. Its components will then be launched into space, to become part of a future star or solar system. The timescale of that thrown stone is strikingly different from our own.

Plate tectonics, the great scientific breakthrough of twentieth-century geology, has nothing to tell us about the visible geology of Cape Cod and its kettle ponds. Upward extrusion at the mid-Atlantic tectonic fault continues to push Cape Cod and North America away from Europe, and rarely a small offshore earthquake is felt in New England. But the creation of the Cape Cod kettle ponds was all done by ice, each in a single moment, without the need for any motion of the vast tectonic plates. They are "fossil icebergs."[1]

Today, almost two hundred centuries after the Ice Age glaciers, the site of the ancient triple-chunk icefall is one of seven ponds on Cape Cod that carries the Long Pond name. Even the islands of Nantucket and Martha's Vineyard have their own Long Ponds. Cape Codders are not known for their innovative place names. (I have read that "Long" is the second-most-common name for a Minnesota lake.) Most folks attach the name of the surrounding Centerville village to the name of our pond, to distinguish it from its nearby namesakes, which also must carry a village namesake to be distinguished from their fellow Long Ponds. Better to my mind would be to give each pond a unique name, honoring its individual value! Our sister kettle pond, Lake Wequaquet, takes its name from the language of the humans who lived on Cape Cod when Europeans first arrived, the Wampanoag. I hope the officials who designate place-names will adopt an appropriate Wampanoag name for Long Pond Centerville someday.

As European immigrants moved in, horse-and-wagon teams trotted by Long Pond on nearby roads and ventured onto its thick ice in winter to harvest chunks of ice for preserving food in ice boxes. An artificial herring run was dug from the Craigville salt marsh to connect to Long Pond, then continued north to the neighboring larger pond, Lake Wequaquet. River herring, introduced or mistaking the new ditch for their birthplace, began to use the man-made stream to spawn each spring. The artificial herring brook, called a "run," goes by the rather grand name of the Centerville River. Like Long Pond Centerville, the herring run also needs a better name, but that can wait for another day.

In the early years of the twentieth century, a few fish camps were built along the delightful shores of Long Pond. The properties and shoreline were surveyed, and its surface area of fifty-one acres was established. Being greater than ten acres, it acquired the ostentatious official title of "great pond" from the state of Massachusetts. The Environmental Protection Agency considers a water body to be a "pond" if it is less than ten acres, and a lake if larger. In the rural Midwest, where I grew up, a pond is a small drinking pool used by livestock, usually a fraction of an acre. But on Cape Cod, most freshwater bodies are ponds. Period.

Most of today's shores are now claimed as property for homes. The town has preserved two access spots for the general public, called "ways-to-water." One features a small swimming beach; the other, a boat launch roadway. Pontoon boats, kayaks, stand-up paddleboards, and canoes ply its waters. Motors greater than ten horsepower and jet skis are mercifully forbidden by local law.

While glaciation made Long Pond and Cape Cod, erosion reforms it daily. On the Outer Cape its effect is most striking. Marconi's original wireless station in Wellfleet, from which president Teddy Roosevelt sent his "most cordial greetings and good wishes" to Britain's King Edward VII in 1903, is long gone, washed into the ocean by aggressive beach cliff erosion. In 1928, Henry Beston spent the year at Eastham, also perched on the edge of the tall dunes, and wrote eloquently about the sea and the beach, its creatures, and his "outermost house."[2] That structure was gone fifty years later, also washed into the ocean.

The land at the "elbow" and the "fingertips" of the Cape arm at Chatham and Provincetown are not glacial but drifted sand, pushed there by currents from the Atlantic shores. Home to many waterfowl and seals, Monomoy Island on the southeastern elbow of Cape Cod in Chatham is eroded sand, created after the glaciers departed. Monomoy is cyclically reshaped into a peninsula or an island every few years, as the sand is washed about by storms and currents. Likewise, the tip of Cape Cod at Truro and Provincetown is all eroded sand, not glacial moraine. The entire Atlantic beach section of the Cape between Provincetown and Chatham is narrowing rapidly from erosive processes. The ocean does what it chooses with its sand, at a pace on Cape Cod that often astounds us.

Geologically, the Cape is an island, severed from the mainland by a 150-meter-wide canal that was built in the early 1900s. The Cape Cod Canal is spanned by three bridges and nestled in the natural valley of the Monument River in a route first recommended by Miles Standish and later surveyed by George Washington. It shortens the nautical route between Boston and New York by over one hundred miles and allows ships to avoid the dangerous shoals along the Cape's eastern shore, where hundreds of ships have sunk. As the tides change every six hours, a brisk current appears in the canal between the Cape Cod and Buzzards Bays. Occasionally, a North Atlantic right whale will transit the Canal, and boat traffic halts while all watch out for the whale's safety.

The legacy of the Ice Age moraine, an ancient conglomerate of sand and small stones, is visible where we launch our canoes and kayaks on Long Pond. When I take a paddling excursion, some of these stones, locked together like cobblestones and tightly embedded in the sand, scratch the bottom of my canoe as it leaves the shore. My past efforts to remove the stones have merely freed up more sand to drift away with the waves and expose a new tight matrix of small rocks and sand. The Cape is just a big pile of compressed stones—rocks all the way down—packed into the sand and pockmarked in a single moment by the big icefalls of eighteen thousand years ago. As the canoe scrapes across that rough matrix, I remember that the tight grid of stones has been fixed in place on an incomprehensible timescale, much different from my own.

2

Aquifer
Water Level Theater
~

bright clear autumn days
second summer is here
the Cape's best season

Living adjacent to a freshwater lake is delightful, watching the four seasons, changing weather, diverse waterfowl, and human activities. Thoreau considered lakes to be the landscape's most expressive feature. We see that feature played out daily at Long Pond. For us, a substantial bonus is also living next to the manmade herring run where it makes its southbound exit from Long Pond. It flows along our east property line and straight down to the salt marsh, a half mile from us. Directly across the lake, on the north shore, we can see where the herring run enters, bringing water and herring down from the higher elevation at Lake Wequaquet, a quarter mile north of us. Watching the lake and the run change day by day, through the year, is endlessly entertaining.

For 99 percent of its existence, Long Pond had no stream access in or out. Our small herring brook above and below the lake barely changes that fact. Only the narrow watershed around the circumference of Long Pond drains runoff surface water into the pond. Its watershed is not linear, as we find around streams and rivers. Some kettle ponds have steep banks, which we have only along the western shore of Long Pond.

The Cape's underground aquifer migrates downhill from the higher ground west of us, passing through Long Pond on its way. Limnologists (lake scientists) have known from studies decades ago that at least 95 percent of the water that comes and goes from Wequaquet and Long Pond comes from the aquifer, entering and leaving through the bottom of those lakes. Fresh aquifer water completely flushes each lake every few days. The flow from the herring run is trivial by comparison.

A Barnstable town surveyor has placed a water level gauge pole in the lake near our herring run entrance, so the natural resources officers can monitor the lake level and ensure sufficient flow into the herring run for the springtime herring migration. I check it weekly or so, watching the rise and fall as the year passes. I've logged a record of the water level for the five years we've lived here, and online I found fifteen additional years of records. Every few years, lake ice pushes the surveyor's gauge pole over or breaks it in two, so a new survey team must set a new pole and gauge. As I write this, the hapless pole is gone after its destruction by a recent winter ice sheet. Before it collapsed, I noted the level of the top of several nearby shoreline rocks, so the water level records can be kept in an approximate way until the town surveyors provide a new pole and gauge with the warmer spring weather.

Near the gauge pole, at the entrance to the herring run, lie several dozen white plastic sandbags. These are moved around every few weeks by the efficient, pleasant town natural resources officers to control the herring run flow volume, which affects the ability of river herring to migrate up or down. The officers use the lake level shown on the gauge pole to decide how high to stack the sandbags to limit or increase the herring stream flow rate.

Cape Cod's population triples in the summer, and the water use of all those visitors often drains the aquifer faster than summer rain showers can fill it, so the aquifer level and the water level in Long Pond usually drop. In winter, the rains and fewer water users replenish the aquifer, and its level rises, pushing upward the water level of the invisible aquifer and, as a result, of Long Pond. The herring fry prefer to leave in the fall, but do just fine here over the winter if they are trapped by a low water level and dry herring run. They leave for the ocean when the water is moving in the run again in the springtime.

Lake Wequaquet has a water gate with adjustable boards to regulate herring run flow between there and here. The town natural resources officers monitor those boards and our sandbags for the best interests of the herring. Some citizens who live nearby believe the boards and sandbags set both the lake level and the groundwater level, which are really controlled by the aquifer. When their basements are wet, those misinformed folks want the officers to remove boards or sandbags, hoping it will lower the groundwater level. The sandbag and board movement is "water level theater," drama and acting but no progress on the groundwater problem. What really needs to happen to reduce basement water is honest dialogue and better building permitting of the depth that basements are dug over the aquifer. In an unusually dry year, a basement may be dug deeply without flooding. But in wet years, there will be aquifer water there. That basement water is not from Long Pond nor Wequaquet, which are merely reporting the aquifer level, not dictating it. Moving the boards and the sandbags is useful only for changing the flow in the herring run, not for draining either the lake or nearby wet basements. That fact has been known for decades.

The most common water surface levels for our lake in Centerville are twenty-five to twenty-seven feet above sea level. Long Pond's water does fall below the lowest mark on the gauge pole, which is twenty-five feet and two inches. Several times there has been a six-foot patch of dry ground around the bottom of the pole, so the water level of Long Pond could only be estimated for my records. The herring run goes dry and ceases to flow, sometimes for months. An island of dry sand appears at the north herring run around its entrance to the lake, like a dry river delta. How low has Long Pond been in the past eighteen thousand years? Could the entire pond have ever dried up? The western United States is suffering its worst drought in twelve hundred years, which is only a few percent of eighteen thousand post–Ice Age years. Climate change in geological timescales may have some future surprises for us.

When the water level is low, we have a wide sandy beach along our Long Pond shore. A tight grid of stones is exposed, grouted with tan-colored sand. It is harsh on the bottom of the canoe, no matter how carefully I climb in and launch. When the water level comes back up, the water laps on the edge of the vegetation, and provides a softer, smoother place to launch and land the canoe.

In those eighteen thousand years that Long Pond has held water, leaves and branches and dead lake plant and animal inhabitants have accumulated on the bottom. I can imagine it would fill up the pond, seeing the blizzard of autumn leaves that find their way into the water each year. But core sampling of other Cape kettle ponds does not show much shallowing from new layers of organic matter. The depth testing of Long Pond reveals its deepest spot is along the north shore, reaching about twenty-five feet. Most of the eastern lobe of the lake is ten feet deep or less. Some Cape Cod kettle ponds are more than fifty feet deep, while Walden Pond is over one hundred feet deep, the deepest kettle pond in Massachusetts.

Kettle ponds across North America are known by scientists to be superb preservers of the pollen record. Most trees and grasses scatter their pollen into the air rather than depending on pollinators like bees. That pollen may blow for miles, even hundreds of miles. A durable polymer coat protects each grain of pollen until it lands. And even after sinking to the bottom of a kettle pond, it may be preserved in layers for thousands of years.

From high above, our lake has the shape of a bowtie, with three distinct but connected round sections. We live on the south shore of the middle section, the bottom of the knot of the bow tie. The west lobe is the largest and has a small thumb-shaped bay on its north side. Water lilies live there, showing their large white flowers each summer. They do not seem to be spreading to other parts of Long Pond, as they have at nearby Red Lilly Pond, which has dense stands of lily plants. Perhaps we can give the muskrats some credit for eating our lilies and controlling them.

During our successful herring migration count a few years ago, we got some additional attention for our herring run. Three US Fish and Wildlife Service guys came by to see the run and discuss upgrading the ramshackle plastic sandbag system for regulating water flow. They proposed a more substantial and permanent water-flow-regulating system, which would make it easier for the town's natural resources officers to facilitate water flow and the herring traffic. The FWS people were very upbeat and friendly. Meanwhile, the herring were splashing and chasing each other nearby. If we get their engineered gates, I hope that they will not be used for water-level theater, as our sandbags and the wooden gate up at Wequaquet have been.

3

Herring Run
Highway for an Epic Migration
~

sunrise herring watch
cacophony fills the air
joyous symphony

When we retired to Cape Cod in 2017, my wife Jane and I found that being adjacent to a herring run was one of the aspects of our cottage grounds that created the greatest joys. During the first two years, we carefully (but irregularly) watched for the springtime herring migration without seeing one herring. From the abundance of herring during Pilgrim days up through the 1960s to such an eerie absence then made us surprised and sad.

In springtime, the herring stream's flow is brisk but shallow—rarely more than a foot deep and only six to ten feet wide. The babbling brook carries sticks and leaves away, along with an occasional frisbee or tennis ball badly tossed for our Labrador retriever. We hope most of the thrown debris travels out of the run and does not obstruct the passage of the river herring on their springtime spawning mission.

According to a book of the detailed history of Barnstable, our herring stream was dug by "unemployed Civil War veterans" and their horse teams in 1867.[1] With their shovels, the veterans dug a wide ditch up from the salt marsh to Long Pond, then on up to Wequaquet. The Long Pond watershed changed from a thin perimeter around the pond to the common linear shape we find with most river watersheds. The future herring run took the august name Centerville River and the town of Barnstable paid for it. A town official and others had organized a new fishing company at Wequaquet in 1860, but that may just be a coincidence, not corruption. In another story in the same history book, we read that the lower half of our run, below Pine Street, was dug "in the early part of the 17th century."[2] This seems doubtful to me. Centerville was barely settled by Europeans at that time. The section below Pine Street appears to be a natural drainage gully to me, wisely utilized by the 1867 excavation team for their route to Long Pond. Either way, the history of our artificial herring run is substantial.

The manmade ditch-turned–herring run comes up twenty-five vertical feet in the half mile from the salt marsh, which is also called the Centerville River. The steepest part is the natural gully section below Pine Street. North of Long Pond, the excavated streambed continues gently and artificially straight as an arrow for a quarter mile and eight vertical feet up to Lake Wequaquet.

The natural resources officers walk down the entire herring run to the salt marsh early each spring, systematically trimming and removing obstacles to herring migration. I bought some high-top rubber Wellington-style for occasional forays into the run. If a few branches and vines downstream touch the surface, they can create waves that confuse our herring counting, so I put on the boots and trim them. And retrieve any errant Labrador toys that I find.

In 2020, we again saw no herring on our frequent counting observations, yet the natural resources officers estimated a count of five hundred on our run. On a late-spring day that year, one of the town conservation officers was adjusting the sandbags at our place to change the herring run flow rate. He had seen about fifty herring waiting in the salt marsh to come up our run, and thought they were intimidated because the flow was too fast, so he was slowing it to make swimming upstream easier for them. While we spoke, one herring swam by! It passed very quickly, visible for only a few seconds. The dark gray shape, thin and long with a distinct forked tail, was unmistakable. Our herring count was finally on!

Two fine books about river herring, *The Alewifes' Tale* and *The Run*, have enlightened me.[3] The latter is a 1959 book about the busy run in nearby Brewster. The heroic act of migrating from remote continental shelf waters of the Atlantic Ocean to upstream lakes on Cape Cod carries great risk for the intrepid herring. The purpose of the migration is a mystery. There must be some property of fresh water that makes life safer and easier for spawning or for the early days of the tiny herring fry. Perhaps there is better access to the zooplankton food they need at that stage of life. Certainly, the adult herring make a metabolic shift when transiting from salt water to fresh water, then back again. River herring may live eight years and make their "anadromous" (from the ancient Greek, "running upward") migration several times—if they can avoid the dangers. Salmon make a similar trip, but not on Cape Cod, and only once at the end of life. Eels make the opposite migration trip, leaving the lake as adults to spawn and then die in the ocean, while their offspring make the risky trip across the wide ocean and back up the herring run, arriving with the herring each spring. Biologists call the eel's reverse migration pattern "catadromous" from the Greek for "running down." Many birds and waterfowl migrate to warmer spots for reliable food during the winter months. Many of us humans also migrate to a warmer climate, usually when we grow older and less tolerant of cold weather. I would label that migration catadromous.

The heroic adventure of living for 90 percent of your adult life in the Atlantic Ocean, constantly on the lookout for predators, then swimming over a thousand miles to find the very same tiny stream on Cape Cod where you were born, avoiding the voracious predators at the mouth of the herring run and again at the entrance to Long Pond, then spawning or swimming on up to Lake Wequaquet and spawning there, and finally swimming back down the run and out to sea, again dodging the packs of hungry predators, both in and above the water, then swimming the arduous trip to the deep ocean for another year of staying ahead of predators there—what a wild roller-coaster ride of drama such a life would be!

The river herring genus is thirty-four million years old, more than a hundred times the age of Homo sapiens, and a thousand times the age of Cape Cod and its herring runs. Ancestors must have run up ancient rivers that are now long buried in glacial and mountain sediment. Early ancestors may not have even needed fresh water to propagate. Today, there are two species of freshwater-spawning river herring—alewife and blueback herring, and another species called Atlantic herring, which do not come into fresh water.

There are a lot of differences between the two river herring species, which to outward appearances are nearly identical. The alewife migrate early in the spring when the water temperature in the herring run reaches 51 degrees Fahrenheit; the bluebacks prefer water in the run to warm up to about 57 degrees when they migrate. Judging from the water temperatures in the run, our crowd in early April is presumably alewife, with bluebacks coming a few weeks later. Some of the alewife complete their spawning and are already emigrating back to the ocean when the last of the bluebacks are still coming up. The bluebacks seem more timid, easily scared by my visible presence along or above the run on my counting perch. They often turn back—at least briefly. The alewife usually just press on with vigor. Spawning behavior also distinguishes the two species. Alewife spawn in still water, such as in the pond, while bluebacks prefer to spawn in the running water of the herring run. When blueback herring are predominant, later in the spawning season, we see much more activity along the shore and at the entrance to the herring run—swirling and splashing—as the males nudge the females to encourage them to release eggs. I've not seen any such activity from the alewife; for them this presumably occurs in the middle of the pond, perhaps near the bottom and out of sight.

A group of gulls is often present across the pond, where the herring run enters Long Pond from Lake Wequaquet to the north. We rarely see gulls at the herring run on our south side of the pond, perhaps because we have more overhanging branches or less sunshine. It may be easy for them to spot a herring as it moves across the wide shallow delta of eroded sand on the north side, although watching from the sandbags

A CAPTURE AT THE HERRING RUN

on our side would also seem effective to me (no gull has asked my opinion). On occasion, there has been so much spawning commotion on our side of the pond that a herring gull flies over to check it out. The gulls fly up a few feet, then pounce. They make quite a comical show. Rarely do they come up with a herring, but they repeat the performance often enough to make it worth their trouble. No wonder they are called herring gulls.

In the good old days, the redoubtable herring came in massive waves, so many it was inconceivable that they could ever be endangered. They were harvested by dipping a bucket or net into the stream. The Cape Cod harvest was measured in thousands of fifty-five-gallon barrels of herring, not the individual fish we count today. By my calculation, there were five hundred to one thousand herring per barrel, or one million per thousand barrels. The actual count on our Centerville run in 2021, according to calculations by the state marine fisheries statistician, was about two hundred thousand, or a few hundred of those old-fashioned barrels.

A dear friend remembers standing in the waters of the north side herring run in the 1960s as a seemingly infinite number of herring swarmed around her legs. There are legends about busy workmen on the job in those days dropping their tools and running for their fishing gear when someone shouted, "The herring are running!" We heard such stories when we lived on Lake Wequaquet with Jane's parents in the early 1970s. How easy it was to fool ourselves into thinking that such plenty then meant that there was an inexhaustible supply. Like with the slaughter of the bison, otter, and beaver, we humans were fooled. Our treatment of ocean fish today implies that we did not learn our lesson.

When the herring migrate up the run, we usually see a steady stream of singles or small groups, as many as twenty. We've seen schools of two hundred, but those are uncommon. When they come to a dark tunnel, like the culvert under

Pine Street or Phinneys Lane, they stop and swirl back and forth, waiting for one heroic herring to lead the entire school (called an "army") through the dark narrow passage. If they are migrating at night, as they usually do on our run, they may encounter my flashlight beam as I count them. They may turn back until they can gather their courage and sufficient numbers to zip by the scary light.

By late May, we see almost no upstream herring activity on our run. At the north shore entrance of the run from Wequaquet down into Long Pond, I may see one blueback herring zipping back and forth, moving very fast. Then four, then five, then ten, all moving up and down the run at a brisk pace, rarely traveling more than fifty feet before turning around. They are no doubt spawning bluebacks. Quite enthusiastic, the males nudge the females to get them to release the eggs, which the males then fertilize in the water. One female can release 100,000 eggs. Later, an army of perhaps two hundred herring arrive along the shore, swirling with their dorsal fins breaking the water, like a school of miniature sharks. They swim into the run and push upstream. Many pass within a few feet of the canoe. About fifty feet up the run, a great deal of splashing and swirling occurs. Then they all swim out of the run and disappear into the deeper waters of the lake. A minute later, a group of ten do the same, followed in a few minutes by a repeat performance by a larger army of twenty. Once one exuberant fellow flipped onto the shore and was unable to flip himself back in, so I got out of the canoe (got my feet wet) and helped him. He shook himself off and swam out into the lake after his schoolmates.

Our Labrador, Rosie, learned to watch for herring in 2021, and sometimes she alerts us to moving fish. The natural resources officers were glad to hear that some adult herring spawn in Long Pond and likely breed here, rather than all going on up to Wequaquet, where they must pass over the wooden gate. With all the noise we've heard, 2021 was a bigger year for herring than recent years, and not just due to our recent discovery of an annual phenomenon. The lower count in 2022 affirms this hypothesis.

The herring eggs that are not eaten hatch in a few days, and the schools of tiny shiny fry are visible from my canoe, both along the shore and in the middle of the pond. On a late summer day when Long Pond is smooth and quiet, the shiny-silver herring fry can be seen jumping and marking the mirror surface. Some schools of fry are black, likely bass or green sunfish. The river herring fry remain in our lake until late fall, gaining strength for their first journey to the forbidding Atlantic waters.

After the spring emigration of adult herring, the aquifer level usually drops and the herring run can be completely dry. In the past seventeen years, it was dry for parts of five different years. The adult spawning herring stay only for six weeks, so have already returned to the ocean before the aquifer and herring run levels drop. Their offspring, the fry, must adjust to the low water levels, and some years they are trapped for the winter in Long Pond when their exit route is dry. They tolerate cold water very well, as the Atlantic Ocean temperature is often the same as our lake water in winter. We presume the emigrant fry pass a quiet winter on the bottom of the pond, then escape as soon as the water rises and the herring run begins to flow again in the spring. Their survival rate to return to Long Pond to spawn is a fraction of 1 percent.

When the fry decide to leave, what appears to be a million may leave Long Pond at once. We have seen such massive schools depart. If the herring run flow is low, the town natural resources folks remove more sandbags to increase flow. Once, after such a departure of fry, we saw them soon streaming back up the run into Long Pond, in schools of one hundred and larger. Thinking there must be some obstacle downstream, Jane told the natural resources officer, and he investigated it. Soon the fry left again, this time for several years.

A fisheries professional from the state marine fisheries agency has visited our run to consider the placement of an automatic fish-counting machine. He has seemed gruff on e-mail but has a good reputation with the town natural resources officers. He explained the complexity of automatic counters. They are designed for larger fish, like salmon, and may count two adjacent river herring as one. When herring go back and forth, as we have seen them do, the electronic counter registers a count in both directions. The alewife herring may be exiting before the last of the blueback herring arrive. A trial on the Monument River, just off the Cape, showed a careful visual count by humans to be double what the automatic counting device registered. There are video counters, but that requires many hours of tedious video watching, more than most state professionals or herring run volunteers can provide.

An automatic counter might clarify the relative abundance of night migrators compared to those we see during the standard daytime hours, so I'd like to supplement the visual counts with an electronic counter for a season or two. It could also be useful for clarifying how many of our herring travel on up to Wequaquet, compared to those who stay and spawn in Long Pond. Those questions must wait for better technology and a future day.

When the signal to return to the ocean arrives, there is a rush for the exit. Adult herring are visible to us coming down from Wequaquet to Long Pond. Soon afterward, herring are swirling under our pondside bushes, and a huge energetic army is at the sandbags by our run's entrance, ready to leave the pond for the sea. I sometimes paddle the canoe to the herring run entrance to get a closer look, and the schools of herring pass briskly under the canoe and speed off down the run. Two more big schools may pass by in the subsequent half hour. Jane has counted seven big schools in one afternoon, literally thousands heading downstream. We have a patch of clear sand on the herring run bottom just below the sandbags, and it gives us good contrast for counts from our porch. We have seen it turn dark with exiting herring. They often swim up to the gap in the sandbags, then passively allow the current to pull them into the stream. The warm lake water of late May could be stimulating them to leave. They certainly have some astonishing senses, to find the run to their birthplace after years, then to wait for a specific temperature to come up the run. They are very timid and may turn back suddenly, but eventually most of them make their way back to the middle of the Atlantic Ocean for another thrilling year of predator avoidance and filter feeding. What an adventure.

Soon after the herring leave, the lake surface becomes covered with oak pollen, so thick the leeward shoreline can take on a lime-green hue. The water temperature at this time of year is nearly 70 degrees, and the green sunfish (*Lepomis cyanellus*) are clearing their nests, forming three-foot-diameter round spots in the shallow areas of the pond. I have counted over one hundred such nests around the shoreline of Long Pond. The big eighteen-inch-long bass we see at the top of the herring run, in groups of as many as six, deposit their eggs in underwater grass in shallow water, without clearing a nest. Soon fry from both species will be swarming around the pond.

One of the features of our cottage property that has most delighted us is the herring run, and observing it and learning from it has exceeded our anticipation. Having a babbling brook along one side of our property is peaceful and beautiful. The fact that the brook hosts an epic annual migration of thousands of heroic ocean fish to their spawning waters is exhilarating.

From the abundance of herring during Pilgrim days through the 1960s to their apparent absence in daylight observations during our first three years on the run to the robust counts of the past two years—the herring run of Long Pond and its river herring have educated and thrilled us.

4
Counting Herring
Come and Go

~

fast darting herring
show dark against the tan sands
like little torpedoes

When the annual Cape Cod river herring run featured billions of vigorous adult herring, surging in endless schools over every obstacle, there seemed to be no reason to attempt to quantify them—other than financial accounting of the barrels of dried fish shipped to hungry customers off the Cape. As the numbers dramatically tapered in the 1970s, concern arose. There was a clear need to determine year-by-year changes and trends in herring populations and to clarify the reasons for and extent of their decline. Citizen volunteers joined the survey, as the state marine fisheries agency's manpower was too low to accomplish such a time-intensive task.

The fisheries scientists tell us the alewife migrate in from salt water when the freshwater temperature reaches 51 degrees, which in most years is in early April. The pond's water cycles between about 40 degrees in January and February, to 50 in April, 60 in May, and 70 in June, and then peaks in July and August in the low 80s. Beginning in September, the temperature falls at the same rate—from 70 to 60 degrees in October, to 50 in November, and 40 in December. The highest temperature that I've recorded in five years is 84 degrees, and the lowest is 36. Snow on the ice can absorb sunlight and warm the top layer of water, but there is usually little temperature variation with depth. The wind and waves mix the cold and warm water well, all the way to the bottom of our shallow pond. Deeper ponds can have stratified colder water, called thermoclines, but Long Pond is shallow enough to likely have a homogeneous temperature.

Today, volunteers count the migrating herring in about two dozen streams on Cape Cod each spring. Ours is the only artificial herring run on the Cape, although others have man-made infrastructures, such as fish ladders and dams. A nonprofit organization, the Association to Preserve Cape Cod (APCC), has taken responsibility for compiling the Cape-wide herring count. The APCC recommends starting the count on April 1. A statistician from the state marine fisheries agency takes the raw data compiled by the APCC from all the runs on the Cape and determines an "actual" count, including those herring that passed when no one was looking. To extrapolate from observed counts to actual values, the counts must be performed in a rigorous statistical fashion. A counting volunteer must count the passing river herring for exactly ten minutes at least three separate times in each four-hour block between 7 a.m. and 7 p.m. When the herring come up in large numbers, stopping the count at ten minutes is difficult. But those are the rules. The total count is ninety minutes of observation each day, rain or shine, for two months. In 2021, the sheer numbers were so exhilarating that we did not want to limit our counting to a ten-minute stretch. But to continue would mess up the statistics, as the second count would not be random.

When the ten-minute count is zero, as it most often is, the watching is less exciting. April and May on Cape Cod can be more like late winter than early summer. In order to not miss any early migrants, Jane and I start looking around March 15. It may be overcast and drizzling with a brisk wind blowing out of the north and an air temperature below 50 degrees. Ten minutes pass slowly when standing outside on such a day! I must come inside to warm up between counts, which fits best with the recommended protocol in addition to resuscitating me. We have a corner window on our screen porch that looks down on a sandy stretch of the run, where the dark bodies of the herring contrast with the tan color of the sand and can often be accurately counted from indoors. I have cleaned off some of the fallen leaves in that sandy patch of the run to improve the contrast for our counts. On cold and rainy nights that spot on the porch is a fine place for counting with a bright flashlight.

Another fine spot to count in nice weather is on a large old stump, left from cutting a rotting oak tree that loomed ominously over our garage. The stump almost overhangs the run, about ten feet above it. We have dug a few steps from the top into the bank down to the stump. Standing there one can see one hundred yards down the straight run toward the south, the salt marsh, and the upstream herring schools.

During the eight weeks of the herring migration, I often get up to count in the wee hours in the dark, as our population of herring seems to prefer migration during that time. When they silently swim by in the dark, their gray silhouettes in the flashlight beam appear to be "ghost fish," coming back to their old haunts. Eerie, light, floating along against the current with little effort. Jane often does the sunrise counts, as she is a better morning person than I am. On the days when I do get up at sunrise, the scenery and the birdsong symphony are spectacular. In the early morning, Long Pond is usually calm, and its surface is like a mirror. Some days there is a lightly moving mist on the smooth pond surface or even fog that may obscure the opposite shore, only two hundred yards away. Audible is the babbling of the gentle waves in the run, which I can rarely hear in daylight hours. The state highway beyond the north shore of our lake is silent, with not even a single passing car. It is remarkable how much noise even one set of car tires makes on the road a quarter mile away across the pond! How accustomed we become to that intrusive noise in daylight. The hush makes watching for herring in the dark with a flashlight much more serene and enjoyable, as small groups of gray fish swim up the run into the pond.

When the river herring swim upstream against the current, they create a bow wave that is visible from a distance. One fish can do it, or an army of many creates an identical single bow wave. It is visible a full minute before the herring fish can be identified. A divine moment. The run is episodically so shallow that the herring splash with their tails as they swim upstream. A friend who is a close observer has seen them turn on their sides to swim through the shallow parts of a stream. Our stretch has not been that shallow during the migration. If the pond is placid when we are counting, the entering schools create a circular wave as they reach the pond through the gap in the sandbags at the entrance to our run. They later make circular waves in the middle of the lake as the schools fan out, and some of their distinctive bow waves at the north run are visible through our bird-watching binoculars.

Legend has it that the forsythia blooms when the herring migrate. They were not yet blooming in 2021 when the first herring arrived exactly on schedule on the morning of April 1, the first day of the official counting season. There were no bass or herons at the run entrance to tip us off. I thought predators were supposed to be so smart! We saw over one thousand herring on that day alone. The herring came up in groups of two to two hundred, not as individuals. They continued to appear in large schools, and by June we had counted nearly ten thousand.

For me, counting the individual fish in groups of three as they pass is a good method. Jane has taken videos on her phone, which she can slow down later for a more accurate count. One of her slow-motion video counts of a large school agreed with my visual count by threes, so the two techniques seem equivalent. Some counting volunteers use clickers to keep track of the herring they see. We have not done that.

During the abundance of the 2021 run, we learned to look before and at sunrise. Our counts were highest in the early morning, zero or small for the rest of the day, and remained low until after midnight. After ten days of similar results, I decided to get up in the dark to look for herring. The first night, the weather was overcast with no moon. A light fog was on the pond. Our Labrador, Rosie, and I went to the edge of the herring run with the flashlight directed at the water. Soon one, then two, and over the next ten minutes, there were a dozen. They must be the first scouts. They were hard to see, as the surface riffles from the wind distorted the flashlight beam and often looked like a speeding herring. Clearly, some do migrate in the dark. On the following night, I got up at 2 a.m. again and saw a handful of herring under a luminous "supermoon." In the early light at 5:30, Jane saw over two hundred in the ten-minute period. We realized that most of our migrants appear in the wee dark hours or at first light, with a few daylight stragglers. After I asked the state marine fisheries statistician about our nocturnal migration, he recommended the inclusion of the night counts in the data for our run, and told me that counters on at least one other Cape Cod run, the Coonamessett River in East Falmouth, have seen a similar nocturnal migration pattern. It may be more common than that, as the standard counting protocol is daylight hours only, so most volunteer counters don't know what they are missing. We are fortunate to live within a few feet of our counting location, so doing wee-hour visits is not difficult. If we had a long walk or drive to the herring run, as is the case with most of the other Cape herring runs, counting at 2 a.m. would be too great of a challenge.

The safety of darkness may remind our herring of home, deep in the Atlantic Ocean. Or the daytime migrants may have been wiped out in pre-1970s harvests, leaving only descendants of those who traveled at night. Those wee hours of the morning are also very quiet, with little human activity as the gray ghost fish slip by. We confirmed in both 2021 and 2022 that the best time to see herring on our run is from midnight to sunrise. That is the likely reason our daylight counts were zero in 2018–20. A close friend who remembers the herring run here from the 1960s recalls that her dad woke her at night to come to see the swarm of herring—millions—come up our herring run. So they have preferred the cover of darkness on this run in the past. Our early morning daylight counts may just be the stragglers from a larger nighttime army.

At the end of the migration season, I plotted the counts we made, and there were clearly two groups—one around April 1, when the water was 51 degrees (presumably the alewife), and a second around April 20, when the water warmed up to 57 degrees (presumably the blueback herring). Both groups traverse the run in much larger numbers in the dark hours before sunrise than they do when the sun is up.

The town natural resources officers thought the count might be higher at high tide, which makes entry into our run from the salt marsh easier. Our data showed no correlation with the tides. I also wondered if the full moon helped the river herring to navigate the run, but there was no change in count near the full moon dates in 2021 and 2022.

When the APCC issued their final Cape-wide results of the 2021 spring count, we had counted the most herring of any run! Our 2022 count, while much lower, was the second highest on the Cape.

Our neighbors from the nearby Red Lily Pond, about a mile away, have done some diligent daylight counting on their herring run near Craigville Beach. The natural resources officers say their run is problematic, with low flow and little vertical drop. They have an old wooden fish ladder that is broken and out of service (the run flows around it now), and some invasive phragmites weeds at their saltwater entrance. They have been told that a new ladder would cost $250,000—and have raised a portion of that. They have done many ten-minute counts but have seen only a few herring in 2021 and 2022. Jane and I hosted a group of four of their volunteer counters at our house. They were thrilled with our setup and the videos of passing herring we showed them, and we determined to cooperate to bring more attention to our efforts. We saw no herring while they were here, but several thousand went downstream fifteen minutes after they left.

In the autumn of 2021, the Red Lily Pond volunteer leader and I presented a public lecture at the Centerville Public Library on the herring runs in our village. I led off and focused on the herring life cycle and our spectacularly successful count. My colleague spoke of the environmental challenges the herring face: shallow water, invasive phragmites in their run and the salt marsh, runoff from septics, and lawn fertilizer. The librarian was thrilled, telling us that we had had the "biggest group since before the pandemic!" in attendance and fifteen more online. Six from the audience volunteered to help with next spring's count.

When the spawning is complete in May and early June, exit activity is feverish. John Hay called this "the rhythm of sufficient numbers"[1] of the alewife herring we have seen leave in the afternoon, peaking near suppertime. A fair portion—perhaps a third—come back up the run briefly, then travel down again with a different, later group. In late May 2021, a series of large schools, more than a thousand alewife, exited the lake day after day. Their out-migration is more visible than their in-migration. A few blueback herring may still be simultaneously coming up and are not intimidated by the downstream transit of their alewife cousins. Our blueback schools seem to prefer to leave in the early morning hours, but that observation is not based on much data.

June 1 was the last official day of herring run counts in 2021. The town natural resources officer said none of the other herring runs were reporting any more herring by then. I sent our fourteen-page spreadsheet of ten-minute count reports (over five hundred observations) to the APCC. When our data was later submitted to the Massachusetts Division of Marine Fisheries, their statistician's calculation for the "actual count" for our run, based on our submitted sample counts, was over 200,000.

After our astonishingly successful count of 2021, we hoped for the same in 2022. Three other neighbors agreed to help with the counting, two from their own property down the herring run, and one who counts from our garden. Jane saw the first herring. The forsythia bloomed and the first migrants arrived on the first of April, each event alerting us to the other. The daffodils were already in bloom, and the crocuses had finished their debut. We have an early azalea that blooms soon after the forsythia. Truly the herring migration comes as the plant life awakens around our cottage. It also harkens to the renaissance of life among the year-round resident fish in Long Pond. After a long cold winter, the freshwater fish come back to the surface and the shallow areas slowly, but when the herring burst into the pond, the other fish species are awake and visible from the canoe as I paddle along the shore.

By April 12, we had counted only six hundred, all between midnight and 8 a.m., compared to 3,500 by the same date in 2021. Jane and I both think the herring run carried more water in 2022 than in 2021, and the deeper herring run masks the bow wave that the incoming herring make. That made spotting them more difficult than in 2021. Of the several dozen night counts, three-fourths showed herring. Jane had even better success with the sunrise counts, seeing 80 percent of our total count. The later daylight counts were positive in only 2 percent of the time periods. Our neighbors down the run, new counters, saw very few, but they mostly counted in daylight. Overall, in 2022 we only saw 20 percent of the previous year's count. Our town natural resources officer thought counts were down at all the runs in Massachusetts. The problem could be the large ocean fishing trawlers, which drag their huge nets and kill many fish they don't want (which are then discarded). Or pollution, or even a herring pandemic. We may see higher counts again in the coming years.

5

Springtime
Awakening and Blooming
~

tall yellow daffodils
open the springtime season
herring follow soon

On our small plot of lakeside forest, springtime appears very gradually. Often it can be cool and overcast into mid-May. Not really winter, but definitely not summer, either. "Sweater weather" in my mind. The snow and ice vanish, but the temperature is slow to rise, and the dreary days intrude on our fervent wish for sunshine and the warm days of summer. I get spring fever before Cape Cod does. The herring are a sublime distraction, and their eight-week spawning season occupies all of the slow transition period. We can expect to have a compensatory mild autumn on Cape Cod, with pleasant weather lingering into October. On balance, that seems like a fair trade for the chilly springtime. And as Wordsworth wrote, we have a crowd of golden daffodils to enjoy.

The surrounding seas, particularly the Gulf Stream waters that come up from Florida, protect us from harsh weather. The highest temperature recorded in the past 130 years for Hyannis is one hundred degrees, and that was one event in the 1940s. Unlike so many places where climate change has recently broken the all-time high temperature records again and again, few of our all-time highs have occurred since 2000. We get only a third of the snow that falls in Boston, less than one hundred miles north of us. The surrounding ocean protects us.

There are some spectacular sunny spring days. The best daily output from the rooftop solar panels on our cottage is usually in late April or May, even though scientists tell us peak solar radiation is closer to the end of June. There are enough gaps in the tree canopy to allow direct sun on planted areas where we have garden crops and native perennial flowers. The perennial daffodils and crocuses are on automatic pilot, sprouting at the earliest possible spring moment. In March we first see crocuses as well as snowdrops. Throughout most of April, the daffodils hold forth with their cheerful trumpets in golden, bicolor, and multiflora colors. Along the herring run, we replaced the preexisting poison ivy and invasive multiflora rose with invited native wildflowers and trees. To allow the soil to digest the old invasive roots, we mulched the ground with wood chips over cardboard sheets. We created borders around our permaculture "guilds" with round river stones. We planted specific perennials that produce food we can eat and companion plants that fix nitrogen and minerals for the benefit of the soil. We compost our kitchen waste, to recycle the nutrients and energy that we've taken from the edible plants. All that work produces a memorable springtime, lovely summer, and delightful autumn in the lakeside cottage forest garden.

All these factors—soil, sun, rain, sea, altitude—combine to create what is called in the wine business "terroir." Cape Cod has a unique ecology, suitable for many plants but often absent of the organic nutrition that make gardens thrive. Jane has been a fantastic gardener of both food and flower crops for our terroir. She knows many specific species. As the snow melts and the first buds appear, she is continuously planting seeds and nurturing seedlings in her greenhouse for transfer outside when the weather is warmer. She has wisely selected perennial flowers that attract pollinators and butterflies, to complement the plants we harvest for our own food.

We struggle with a few pests in our garden, and a few animal competitors. The poison ivy returns from roots or sprouts from seed. Stealthy ground wasps attacked Jane once without warning while she was planting. Rabbits like to nibble voraciously on our crops or flowers or chew the bark of our seedling trees. Chipmunks and squirrels have been voracious eaters, finishing off many tomatoes before we could get to them and cleaning out our sweet potato patch of all but one tiny, and delicious, potato. They will eat squash and pumpkins before they are ripe. Fencing deters the rabbits, but nothing holds back the chipmunks and squirrels. A muskrat climbs the bank from the herring run to also help himself to some of our garden bounty. We've even seen him climb the narrow limbs of a red maple that hangs out from our shore into the lake. He ate some leaves, then stripped off a small branch for a snack later. The river otters come up from the salt marsh and leave the herring run to scratch out a temporary nest in the leaves and pinecones, damaging our garden plants. A mother snapping turtle has laid her eggs in Jane's compost pile.

On a few occasions each year, a rafter (the term for a group) of wild turkeys has wandered in and eaten whatever they encounter, much to our Labrador's consternation. They are descendants of a Central American turkey, domesticated by the Mayas in 300 BC, taken by the Spanish to Europe, and then brought here by the early settlers. In 1784, Ben Franklin wrote that the turkey is a "much more respectable bird" than the bald eagle, lobbying for it to be our national bird. Wild turkeys were nearly extinct in 1900, and there were none in Massachusetts after 1851. Wild turkeys were reintroduced to western Massachusetts in the 1970s, then to Cape Cod in 1989, and by 2022, our estimated Cape population is thirty thousand. They often stop traffic when a group decides to cross the road one by one.

Professor Susan Simard writes eloquently in "Finding the Mother Tree" about how trees cooperate and communicate with each other underground, in a world we largely ignore.[1] Their root tips stretch toward each other, and fungi link them together into a network, sharing chemicals that signal warning or share nutrition. She tells us that the invisible networks are best exemplified by the partnership between a mother tree and her seedlings or between birch and fir. The mother tree selectively shares more nutrition with her offspring than she does with other neighboring trees. Dr. Simard's paradigm can be enlarged to the connectivity of all life, even that which is above ground and mobile. We are all linked and interdependent. There is no real justice until all experience it; there is no genuine happiness until all receive the care and attention they need. When we understand this and use our synergy for progress for every form of life, the world is a much better place. We should mimic the symbiosis of the forest for the mutual benefit of everyone, including all animals and plants.

Springtime reveals new flowers, but also several small boats scattered by the winter winds around the pond, blown or pushed by ice, away from their moorings, half-sunk from the waves. Their owners, with help from neighbors, usually recover them by Memorial Day weekend.

The male ospreys return around Saint Patrick's Day (March 17), staking out a claim on their chosen nesting site, then defending it against later and often larger birds. The females arrive a few days later, ready to begin family life. They stay until late September, with the adults leaving before the fledglings, who need more time to fatten up for the long flight to South America for the winter. When their fish prey go deep in the pond for a winter's sleep, the ospreys must go south to find food.

A redtail hawk often circles over the pond. They are here year-round, and visible before any ospreys return from their southern vacation. The redwing blackbirds may pester them—called "mobbing"—forcing them to fly away to another area to hunt. The small birds also harass the osprey, mistaking it for a hawk that is a threat to their nests. The blackbirds migrate south for winter but are fickle, returning as early as February, when snow is still on the ground.

Forsythia's yellow buds traditionally announce the need to watch for herring, but also for a solitary migrating common loon or pairs of mergansers and bufflehead ducks, perky and energetic. I have seen them pursue a school of herring fry during my midwinter canoe excursions. The diving ducks are all very hardy and soon move on north, leaving the pond to another solitary diving bird, the coal-black cormorant, as well as the year-round residents who feed from the surface—mallards, Canada geese, and mute swans. Many tree swallows dive and soar over the water, taking their insect meals.

As the water warms, mollusk tracks appear in the sand off our shore, creating elegant swirling Arabic-script marks in the bottom sand when they change locations. The muskrats have devastated their population, and probably know to use the tracks in the sand to find their prey. A few mollusks manage to hide successfully, and they are very prolific, so their population will recover.

Long Pond is a popular fishing lake for local residents. I usually do not meet any other paddlers or fishermen on early springtime outings, but later in the year, there will be two or three small fishing boats out at once. About half of our fishermen are lakeside residents, who often use a kayak. Those who do not live along the shores of the pond can launch from either of the two "ways to water" that the town maintains, one of which has boat trailer access. They seem to prefer to fish from a two-seater boat with a small electric motor. Occasionally we see a fisherman casting a line from a dock or the shoreline, but not often. Most are polite and quiet and release the fish they catch. Occasionally I'll find a beer can or plastic lure that has been left, but not too often.

Fishing does not attract me. Working with hooks and long thin lines, struggling with an animal in pain and anxiety, even the casting and waiting—those activities are not my style. I am glad others find peace and pleasure in it, but I prefer to use my hour on the water in quiet observation of the natural world, in paddling as silently and serenely as possible, in taking a break from the electronic intrusions of the modern world, watching the fish, but leaving them alone.

As the evenings get warmer, we often enjoy a lakeside campfire at sunset. It is so natural to find myself sitting quietly, drawn to staring into the gentle flames, lost in thought, or just hypnotized by the fiery action. I feel a deep connection with ancient ancestors who also stared into the flickering flames over the 800,000 years since humans learned to control fire as a tool. We see some of their history in Neolithic cave paintings. Abstract symbols were often drawn along with hunting scenes from the Ice Age, and the meaning of those symbols is slowly unfolding in the light of archeology and shrewd insights. Most of the cave art is in European caves, drawn as human migration out of Africa occurred. Recently the oldest known cave art was found in Indonesia. It seems to share a common origin with art in the French and German caves. There is probably undiscovered cave art in African caves. The reason we find the signs only in caves may be that is where they were preserved, but not the only place they were drawn. The artists were not "cavemen," as they usually lived outside and used the caves occasionally as special sacred places, dark and inhabited by bears, bats, and the unknown. They also had campfires and must have stared into their flames, hypnotized by the magic of the flicker with its brightness and warmth. We share much humanity.

Sunrise and sunset are magical parts of the day throughout the year, but especially in springtime. Pink, orange, yellow, blue, purple, and every permutation. Our porch is positioned to allow us to see both sunrise and sunset in the late spring when the sun has moved to the north. More of the soft yellow light pours into the main room of our house. The glow of the early morning sun off the trees along the far shore shines a golden reflection onto the water. At the other end of the day, we see that sublime mellow light on the tall trees again, reminding me of van Gogh's fascination with the captivating light he found in Provence. That light is so enchanting that we may find ourselves sitting and admiring it from our porch, even if we do need to wear our sweaters.

6

Vegetation

Climax, Invasive, and Endangered

∿

New England maples
gaily colored mountainsides
we have oak and pine

The shoreline of Long Pond is a contiguous oak and pine forest. Settlers cut most of the trees on the Cape in the seventeenth and eighteenth centuries, just as their ancestors had done in England, Scotland, and Ireland. Then the demand for firewood and ship timber waned. The few remaining trees gradually reestablished a niche for themselves. Some species shaded and outcompeted other species to dominate the forest, and a stable "climax" community of trees and plants appeared. For most of Cape Cod and along the shore of the pond, this stable mix is predominantly white oaks and pines, nurtured by our specific combination of sun, temperatures, and rain. On Long Pond, the north (south-facing) shore hosts most of our pines, while the south shore is mostly oaks.

The forest climax process seems counter to the usual method of operation in natural evolution, which results in more species diversity and more complexity. That statement applies broadly, across broad ecosystems, but not locally, where only the fittest species survive to propagate—and is not applicable over the short term, which in the case of the Long Pond ecology is measured in tens of thousands of years.

The tall straight oaks host two species of green lichen on much of their trunks and many of their branches. Several nearby pines and red maples sport a turquoise lichen. The lichen uses the tree for access to sunlight and air. The local lichens stay flat, called "crustose," on the trunk, with small round balls on the high, dead branches and few streamers. Any longer-hanging streamers are shredded by our passing nor'easter storms. As the oaks get older, they accumulate more dead branches, so more sunlight can stream down on the lichen. Some folks believe the lichen hastens an oak tree's death. To assume that events that happen in sequence are part of a causal process is a logic trap to catch us. The Romans had an expression for that human error, *post hoc ergo propter hoc,* meaning "after the fact so due to it." We sophisticated moderns still fall into that trap. The lichen does not harm the oaks. In fact, the lichen absorbs air pollutants, which can kill the tree. Their presence is used as a gauge of air quality. Thus, lichen is less common in urban areas, where the air is less clean. The fact that our oak lichen is so robust is a good sign of the quality of our outdoor air on the seabound peninsula of Cape Cod.

On several of the oaks, a darker green lichen also grows and covers a portion of the turquoise lichen. It is a composite organism, both fungus and cyanobacteria. The bacteria provide photosynthesis, fix nitrogen, and share nutrition with the fungi, and the fungi provide the structure and attachment to the tree. Botanists call the composite organism by the name of the fungus, which is considered the dominant organism. When parties share an ecosystem and cooperate, scientists call that "mutualism." The behavior is being found more and more often in the natural world.

In the South, lichen can grow longer and stringy and become "Spanish moss." However, the name is a misnomer, as moss is a real plant that has its own photosynthetic capacity without having to take on a tenant. Moss is a primitive plant unrelated to lichen, likely an ancestor of modern trees, flowers, and ferns. We have authentic moss along the shores of Long Pond, but it grows on our rocks and on the ground, not on the tree trunks.

Botanical marvels are revealed by the progression of the seasons, changing day length, temperature, and weather. When autumn arrives, the Cape does not get the brilliant colors for which northern New England is famous. The ospreys and hummingbirds disappear to warmer places. The water gets clearer and the squirrels frantically gather acorns. Our lakeside maples that hang out over the edge of the pond, variously called red, soft, or swamp maples, briefly turn fire-engine red before dropping their leaves. Their green leaf pigment, chlorophyll, is broken down into sugars in preparation for a long sleep during winter's chilly, dark days. Two other chemicals in the leaves, carotenoids and anthocyanins, are more stable and remain to reflect yellow or red colors into our eyes. The pines and spruce stay "evergreen" all year. In the autumn, the Virginia creeper vines, occasional sumac trees, and robust poison ivy turn bright red. That chemical signal from the poison ivy is a signal to avoid it or to carefully pull it. Most of the white oak leaves change to a dark rusty brown, which is not striking. They hang on into the colder November winds, then drop to provide springtime cover for the eggs of insects. The other trees drop their leaves for a long period in the autumn. When the leaves fall like rain in the wind, one would think the trees soon would be bare, but the leaf supply seems to be inexhaustible. When we burn the fallen leaves, or blow them into a pile and haul them off, we are destroying important lightening bug habitats. No wonder we rarely see those glorious blinking lights on our warm summer nights! Sixty years ago they were everywhere in uncountable numbers on pleasant summer nights.

Pines are a mix of pitch and Eastern white on Cape Cod. The pitch pine needles grow in clusters of three, while the white pine needles cluster in groups of five. Some that grow too tall or close to the shore can topple into the pond, creating an arch that a shore-hugging canoeist can get under when the water is not too high. There are three such arches on the north shore of Long Pond. One got a companion fallen pine next to it last winter, and that second fallen tree now blocks passage. Further along that same north shore, another pine has been leaning far out over the water for over a year. It held fast at a 45-degree angle for most of last year but now is down to 15 degrees with its roots creating an ever-larger bulge in the uphill ground. The canoe and I detour widely around it or paddle a little faster when passing beneath it, although it is unlikely to fall abruptly after such a long, slow lean.

Long Pond also hosts several rare and endangered native plant species. State inspectors walk the shores every few years to look for three state-listed "species of concern": Plymouth gentian (*Sabatia kennedyana*), redroot (*Lachnanthes caroliniana*), and terete arrowhead (*Sagittaria teres*). All prefer wooded areas and sandy terrain that extends to the shoreline, which they find on the pond's north shore in its unimpeded southern exposure to the summer sun. Two other state watch-list plants, hyssop hedge nettle (*Stachys hyssopifolia*) and rose coreopsis (*Coreopsis rosea*), are also present there. All are damaged by raking the beach, adding sand to the shoreline, mowing to the water's edge, and the storage of boats and docks, which intrude on their habitat. On the last inspection, the state botanist found some of the redroot had been weed-whacked, chopping off the blossoms. At the two sites where the rare plants increased in his census, none of these activities had occurred, showing that humans and the rare plants can coexist.

Purple loosestrife is an invasive weed whose tall red-flower stalks are common around the pond, blooming first on the north shore. We have a few clumps that bloom later in the summer on our north-facing shoreline. Each plant produces millions of seeds. It had taken over the Sudbury River plain in Concord when we lived there thirty years ago. Jane and I think the purple flowers are beautiful when under control, but we pull enough to keep it away from the herring run drainage.

Underwater, Long Pond hosts a variety of pond weeds, several of which are "floating," meaning their leaves may appear on the surface. Scattered among the pond weeds on the lake bottom is quillwort, a hollow-stem plant that does well in Long Pond. The swans and geese pull up the pondweed and eat it, and the quillwort gets pulled as collateral damage. It is discarded and floats in mats to the leeward side of the pond, where it quickly composts.

None of the pond weeds accumulate in sufficient numbers to impede the traffic of the kayaks, pontoon boats, or occasional lake swimmers. But we do host an invasive weed that poses such a threat. Hydrilla is an aquarium plant from south India that was introduced into canal water in Florida sixty years ago, then spread up the waterways of the East Coast. Its first reported sighting on Cape Cod was in our pond in 2001, soon after it was first reported in eastern Connecticut. Even dogs or waterfowl can spread tiny viable fragments from one water body to another, but it usually rides on the propellor of a small outboard motor. This weed spreads by stems, leaves, and root rhizomes, the latter being resistant to treatment. Every year, it must be chemically treated, and then dies back for a while—but only temporarily. The US Fish and Wildlife Service has called it the world's worst invasive aquatic plant and lists it as a federal noxious weed. They recommend boaters clean and dry their boats (including all gear, propellers, and the trailer) when they are pulled out of any body of water with hydrilla, and drain any bilge or motor water before entering a new body of water. But there is no enforcement of that recommendation.

I did not notice it on my canoe sojourns until several years after we moved to our home here. I then found three small, dense hydrilla patches at the southeast corner of the pond, near the small public beach. The hydrilla is brilliant lime green, resembling a fresh Christmas tree resting on the bottom. Later there was also a tiny patch near a wooden dock closer to our home. If the hydrilla infestations were in deeper water, I would not have seen them. I usually paddle within one hundred feet of the shore and cannot identify plants deeper than ten feet most summer days. Some sneaky hydrilla may be hiding in the deeper water.

After the first treatment, the impact was spotty. After several more chemical treatments, the hydrilla slowly lost its Christmas-tree color, taking on a darker, dull tint, with the peripheral areas of each patch looking the worst. Many of the streamers became thin white stems without leaves. Finally, after multiple treatments through the summer, all the hydrilla disappeared.

HYDRILLA WEED

The following year the hydrilla showed up in force again near the east end of the pond, rapidly spreading along the south shore into the middle lobe. A few patches could be seen along the uninhabited east shore and in a few spots along the north shore. By summertime, there were a dozen visible patches of the invasive hydrilla weed along the south shore, from the public beach to within one hundred yards of our cottage. The patches seem to be smaller and newer as one paddles west, so perhaps it spread in that direction, although the prevailing wind most of the year is from the west. I looked carefully for it along the west lobe of the pond, and along the north shore, but did not see any. It certainly implies that the introduction was at the public put-in on the east end, with gradual migration around the pond. So far it has made it only halfway to the west end.

The hydrilla may have been reintroduced, but most likely it emerged from resilient old tubers. It spread like wildfire along the bottom, growing an inch per day, primarily in water three to six feet deep. It has been reported in water up to thirty feet deep, which would include all of Long Pond. Once it reaches the surface, it can spread out into dense mats that choke off all other vegetation and boat use of the pond. It has no known diseases or natural predators, but I think the mute swans do eat it. The patches I see remind me of the spread of an aggressive, metastasizing cancer. Remarkably, hydrilla is still for sale in some aquarium stores, and there is no inspection requirement for boats put into and pull out of our pond. Friends who live on a lake in New Hampshire have a citizen-led inspection program, sort of like our volunteer herring counting groups. I am sure a polite volunteer with no badge or enforcement authority must be gentle when "inspecting" a fisherman's boat or encouraging him to clean it before launching it. The intruder on our Cape Cod climax vegetation has found its niche, and dislodging it seems to be beyond our current capabilities.

7

Water Quality
A Legacy of Casual Behavior

⌒

places close to heaven
ancient Celts had the concept
called them "thin" places

Most of the human body is water. The unique chemical polarity of water makes it an effective solvent and lubricant, and it has had an inextricable relationship with life since its creation. Its transparency provides other values that we treasure. When it accumulates in "thin" places like Long Pond, its spirit restores our souls.

One of the most accurate monitors of water quality is the presence of a diversity of native wildlife. River otters are known to be fickle residents if the water is polluted. Fish populations and diversity are dependent on healthy water with little contamination. We have lots of fish, including some eighteen-inch largemouth bass, and the beguiling ospreys seem to make a satisfactory living using Long Pond for their fish market.

Humans are by far the most effective water contaminators of all living creatures. Water clarity is one way to quantify pollution. Water chemistry scientists distinguish turbidity from clarity. The first means cloudiness—suspended sediment and solids. The latter measures how deeply light can penetrate. Both measures are reduced by intrinsic biological materials like phytoplankton, commonly called algae. As the lake water warms during the summer, the dissolved mineral content also is increased. Unfortunately, as these factors are increasing, the clarity is dropping. Dissolved gases like oxygen are also dropping. This is the source of "dead zones," such as off the Mississippi River delta in the Gulf of Mexico. Low oxygen kills off marine life. We have not had a fish die-off in my years on Long Pond, at least not yet. But these factors reduce our pond's water transparency as the summer arrives, then restore it as the autumn air temperatures cool the lake water down.

The town health department measures water quality and clarity twice each year on Long Pond. We assist the town scientist, who comes to our shore with her water-testing kit. We hop into our transparent-hull, two-person kayak that Jane bought. With the clear hull, we can see downward without having to lean over the gunwale, as we do in an opaque fiberglass canoe. We use a round water-clarity-measuring device called a "Secchi disc," colored yellow and black, twenty centimeters in diameter, and attached to a long string. The disc rotates as it descends, so the yellow and black colors alternate. I lower it from our watercraft for the town water scientist, and she notes the depth when the disc disappears. Then I pull it slowly up, and she notes the depth when the disc reappears. The average of those two measurements is a standardized gauge of clarity, first used in Italy in 1865. When we measure clarity on the pond, the values follow a "U"-shaped trajectory through the year, with deeper readings (clearer) in the springtime and autumn, and shallower (cloudy) in the summer. The clear water in spring and fall is considered oligotrophic, with low nutrient and low algae density. The turbid water of summertime has more nutrients and more algae growth. Plants and sediment from rain can also reduce clarity but are not major factors on Long Pond. We get Secchi disc readings between seven and twenty feet (the deepest spot is only twenty-five feet deep). Crater Lake in Oregon has a reading of nearly 130 feet, and some readings in salt water have been over two hundred feet. As an ophthalmologist and vision scientist, I know that humans can see an eight-inch disc at such a remote distance in a crystal-clear fluid, even though it seems like a fantasy.

The US Geological Survey also measures the quality of water in our pond. Annually one of their scientists comes to our herring run, measuring flow, water pH, and other factors that indicate the health of the lake and the run. They record the data and share it with me, but volunteer little interpretation or trend commentary. The National Oceanographic and Atmospheric Administration also collects data, using photos taken by their Landsat satellites. For two years the organization has encouraged citizen scientists to measure the water clarity with the Secchi disc on days when one of their satellites passes overhead, to attempt to correlate those two measurements. We participate and send them our Secchi data.

We have also used a pool chemical test kit to measure pH, nitrite, ammonia, and phosphate levels. The phosphate is the nutrient that scientists think most contributes to the annual harmful algae bloom in Long Pond and other fresh water, while nitrogen is the main culprit in poor water quality in the salt marsh and bays of Cape Cod. Both come from septic leakage.

Another water quality challenge we face at Long Pond is PFAS. This family of thousands of manmade chemicals has been commercially produced since 1949. The US Navy discovered its value in firefighting on ships at sea. Soon it became standard practice to use it in firefighting training, and Cape Cod had two sites over the aquifer recharge zone where that happened for years. One of the Cape Cod training sites was on the military base, and the other was a municipal site. Both are located over our single-source drinking water aquifer, and

contamination of nearby wells has also been found. By the time
the EPA began investigating the harm that PFAS chemicals
may cause to humans, over fifty years of wide use had trans-
pired. Now we know PFAS is a "forever" chemical, persistent
in groundwater, and has been associated with cancers, endo-
crine disorders, and other diseases. A wiser regulatory system
would require a chemical to be proven safe before use, not
wait until human damage and drinking water contamination
has occurred. We have a home water filter to limit our intake
of PFAS chemicals and other pollutants from the town water.
There must also be PFAS in Long Pond, a result of the eastward
aquifer flow, but it is considered to be at a "safe" level. I doubt
that we have the long-term data to be confident of that label.

Having more than fifty homes around the shore of Long
Pond is another ominous situation for our sandbar ecology.
Cape Cod has been very slow to mandate sewage treatment, so
some of the neighbors still have cesspools—nineteenth-century
technology. Others have septic tanks but have neglected to
have them maintained every few years. All these old-fashioned
and dysfunctional systems discharge sewage, which seeps into
the groundwater and then into the lake. The algae we see each
summer is primarily an ancient bacteria known to scientists as
cyanobacteria. They require nutrients to create an overgrowth,
called a "bloom," and phosphate from the sewage diffusion is
their main food. Many of our lakeside neighbors also use lawn
fertilizers, both phosphate and nitrogen, which run off into
the pond with the rain. The response is a robust growth spurt
bloom for the algae in our lake each summer in recent years.

Algae are part of the complex microscopic life that bodies
of water support. Most of the creatures are plankton, from the
Greek word for "drifter." They drift with the currents. Some
plankton are capable of photosynthesis and feed themselves.
These are called phytoplankton. Cyanobacteria fit into this
group. Other plankton are tiny animals and crustacean larvae

called zooplankton. They feed on the phytoplankton, using the energy created by photosynthesis for themselves. The zooplankton are not algae. Our river herring are filter feeders and primarily eat the zooplankton. So on up the food chain.

A "harmful algae bloom" can produce a chemical toxin that is fatal to dogs and people. Cyanobacteria in the public water supply killed seventy-five patients at a Brazilian dialysis unit in 1995. The presence of the toxin is harder and more expensive to detect than the presence of the algae themselves, so we get reports of the latter, without assurances of whether any real toxin danger is present. Technology will address that weakness in the coming years. Lots of data show why algae blooms occur, and that closure to swimming reduces lakeside property values.

In late June in recent years, I can see the floating particles of cyanobacteria in the clear water from the canoe, rarely in sheets on the surface. The appearance of the particles coincides with the town health department's notices of microscopic algae in their testing, and the resultant closure-to-swimming warnings posted at both of the pond's public access points. Our lake association sends out a warning e-mail. The suspended cyanobacteria lower the water clarity in most places, although not uniformly. It can bring a greenish tinge to the water. I can still see pond weeds eight feet down or deeper, so it does not make a huge difference to clarity, but it is noticeable. Some neighbors have floating inflated swim islands out, ready to entertain their grandchildren. They may not be aware of the danger. I warn them from the canoe when I can get their attention.

By August, when the water temperature is over 80 degrees, the cyanobacteria have used up enough of the phosphate and nitrogen nutrients to fade away without treatment. The toxin may be released as the algae die, a risky period for swimmers, primarily dogs and children. The death and decomposition of the algae also use up suspended oxygen in the water, creating a potential suffocating fish kill. We have not had that.

The earth's early atmosphere did not have oxygen in significant amounts until ancient cyanobacteria evolved photosynthesis, which produces oxygen from carbon dioxide. After a billion years, the earth's primordial atmosphere contained only 4 percent oxygen (not enough for most life), but with cyanobacterial help, that rose to 20 percent, where it remains today. So we can thank cyanobacteria for our human life, as well as our algae blooms.

"Algae" is one of the sloppiest words in the English language. In its strict meaning it is a simple, nonflowering, aquatic plant that contains chlorophyll but lacks true stems, roots, leaves, and vascular tissue. Naturally growing seaweeds are algae and are an important source of food in Asia. They provide a wide variety of vitamins and minerals. Fish oil contains omega-3 fatty acids, but the original omega-3 source is microalgae, which are eaten by marine life such as copepods and passed up the food chain through the small filter-feeding fish to us. (That is why it is better for humans to get their omega-3 supplements from seaweed, not millions of tiny fish who have eaten seaweed.) Algae has the potential to produce more biomass per unit surface area in a year than any other form of life. Sewage can be treated with algae, reducing the use of large amounts of toxic chemicals that would otherwise be needed. Algae can be used to capture fertilizers in runoff from farms. When subsequently harvested, the enriched algae can then be used as an organic fertilizer. Many great social problems can be solved with the effective farming of algae. We can hope our descendants use algae more wisely than we have.

Algae can grow on the invasive hydrilla leaves, and protect them from treatment. So the company that treats our hydrilla must wait for the cyanobacteria to wane before it can treat the hydrilla. A toxic partnership. Keeping Long Pond as a thin place will require improved water quality and better control of our unwelcome guests.

8

Ice

Through Thick and Thin

~

smooth sheet of glaze ice
too thin to traverse today
sleepy fish beneath

The north shore of Long Pond Centerville must have been a stunning scene eighteen thousand years ago. A vertical mile of ice dominated the horizon, with waterfalls pouring off at many angles, and occasionally a city-block-sized serac falling off to create a kettle pond like the one I now share with my neighbors. The earliest native Americans may have seen some of those spectacular sights as they first moved into Cape Cod. Its water today follows the same laws of physics as the ancient glacier ice, and it freezes over in various shapes and thicknesses each winter.

A neighbor who grew up along the pond's shores and is now one hundred years old remembers the days before refrigerators, when strong men cut square chunks of thick lake ice to sell for local icebox use. She watched them walk out onto the lake ice, drill holes, then saw between the holes to create the ice chunks. They then used horses and sleds to haul the thick chunks of ice to a cool shed for safe storage. Some of that ice was still around in iceboxes in August, when it was essential for making ice cream or keeping foodstuffs safe from the summer heat.

In the era of climate change, the lake ice is rarely thick enough to cut into blocks. We've seen ice fishermen out on the lake in several of the recent winters. Last winter the ice came and went four different times. We did not ever have enough ice to support a person. My fourth great-grandfather died after he and his team of horses went through the Lake Ontario ice in 1805. I shiver when I think of his experience.

Ice is frozen water, but the physics is not that simple. In nature, where water usually forms hexagonal crystals as the air temperature slowly drops, the frozen water can be snow, hail, or the solid surface of wintertime Long Pond. It takes its whitish or bluish appearance from bubbles or impurities. It is notably slippery, but the physics of that is not worked out. Early theories had ice skates melting a tiny layer of water, due to pressure effects. That idea has lost favor among scientists, but no alternative has taken its place. We see talented figure skaters and hockey players working their magic on the slick surface, but we can't fully explain the physics of that remarkable activity.

Ice has enormous power. As a glacier, it can carve granite into the shape of Yosemite Valley and push up moraines the size of Cape Cod and Long Island. Even a cup of water can break a glass jar as it freezes, since it reaches maximum density at 39 degrees Fahrenheit (4°C), then expands almost 10 percent as it chills to 32 degrees and freezes solid. That's why we have frost heaves on our roadways, and why water in the small cracks in a stone can fracture it to pieces. Solid water is lighter than liquid water, and it floats on liquid water. Those perfect ice crystals expand as water freezes, allowing icebergs to float. Few other natural materials have that same property. A remarkable substance in so many ways!

The ice sheet broke off the depth gauge pole in the lake last winter, and the ice also dislodged my water thermometer, attached to a separate pole stuck in the sand. It was roped to a wooden float to keep it out from the shore, so it was washed into the herring run and floated a distance down the run. I tried to wade in in my Wellington boots and rescue it, but the water was too deep. Eventually, I snatched it with the extendable pole of our tree trimmer. This winter it floated into the run and disappeared.

Winter on Cape Cod often includes nor'easter windstorms, which blow out of the northeast, as their name implies. We have seen a neighbor's boat drift free across the lake in the wind and ice, not to be retrieved until the following Memorial Day. Last winter we saw a loose aluminum rowboat near the north shore herring run entrance, high-centered on the shallow sand. It later blew away across the ice to a secure shoreline niche. On windy days, we watch the imprints of the wind as it whips across the open stretch, called the "fetch," to the northeast— about a quarter mile. Our two big deck chairs have been blown completely off the porch. Lots of limbs and branches come down, and we sometimes lose power for a few days. We have a warm pellet stove, but it has an electronic ignition, so we installed an old-fashioned wood stove in the basement that warms the house when we have no power.

The wind has also shredded our two strings of colorful Tibetan prayer flags. Those same flags in my backyard in Washington, DC, reminded our elderly neighbor of an old-time gas station, and I see the resemblance. Surrounded by tall trees, Long Pond is like a basin, where winds can be trapped and create eddies along the shoreline. I've stopped the canoe in the past and let the wind blow me. Sure enough, the boat traces a circle, as if I had pulled up in the eddy of a large river of wind.

The aquifer water temperature has an impact on our lake ice. When the air temperature is cold for days and snow falls, the lake seems resistant to icing over. I monitor the water temperature near the herring run entrance. Usually, the low for the winter is about 40 degrees. I suspect the ground-warmed aquifer water keeps our lake temperature milder than it would be if air temperature were the only factor. The water near the herring run rarely freezes. Even the small water flow is sufficient to keep the water surface liquid and give the hardy ducks some room to peck and hunt for food. The herring run itself has never been frozen since we moved here five years ago.

The water temperature in the pond is coldest in January, February, and March. Those months are the ones when we often get some patches of ice or even a shore-to-shore freeze. During particularly cold days, ice can gather on each twig and branch that touches the water, forming shiny thumb-sized globular clear crystals that capture sunlight and reflect it brilliantly. As I paddle along in the canoe on such days, a thick down vest beneath my lifejacket, those brilliant crystal globules sparkle at me. When the lake ice is thin, it too is clear and shiny in the glare of the cold sun.

As ice shifts in the wind, it often forms long cracks and even ridges where the large sheets push against each other like tectonic plates. On several occasions there have been dozens of round holes in the ice, resembling impact sites, as if some young boy had thrown big rocks through the slush. Scientists call these "lake stars," and at our pond, they may be randomly scattered every ten yards or so across the entire lake, with granular pieces of ice splashed around their edges. Warm water bubbles from decomposing organic matter on the bottom of the lake rise and break the slushy ice open, and the splashes around the rim of the hole freeze and appear as if the ice was thrown upward from a projectile impact. The whole process is remarkable. We've seen an ice sailboat on our small lake only once, and we do see ice fishermen on occasion. Those lake star holes could be a problem for either group.

Ice continues to play a vital role in the annual cycle at Long Pond, as it did during the kettle pond's creation eighteen thousand years ago. Whether the first North Americans witnessed that creation or not, we can appreciate its enduring role in the lake ecology. Whether or not any ice boxes are still in operation, we can remember how ice continues to shape and enrich the nature of the pond today.

9

Fair Winds and Following Seas

Moving Meditation

~

light southerly breeze
wide blue vistas on each side
silent canoe glides forth

Friends in US Navy communities greet departing colleagues with a wish for "fair winds and following seas," a traditional nautical good luck blessing given as one departs on a voyage on the seas of life. The term is also used at transition ceremonies such as commissioning a ship or an officer, retirement, change of command, and farewells. That fond wish comes to my heart when paddling across the placid pond. If a fair wind is pushing me gently along, whispering in my ears, it keeps me connected to the environment and in the moment. No worrying about the awful pandemic or political news. Only the here and now of the paddle and the pond. Canoeing on such a day can be one out of the playbook of paradise. On such days, I often set out in the canoe to explore Long Pond.

In our hectic, deadline-driven world, the value of quiet is priceless. Few scenes are as calming as a still, silent pond, mirroring the reflected distant shore. To enter that world in a canoe is an experience I treasure. Silently pulling a paddle and traversing a Cape Cod lake is serenity. If I have following seas, they carry me along effortlessly, sometimes briskly. It can be a giddy sensation, riding a roller coaster. On other days the canoe seems like a wind magnet, attracting the headwinds. The winds sometimes seem to come from all four points of the compass, changing faster than I can change my direction of travel on a circuit around the lake. I try to plot a course to enjoy the tailwind and not struggle with the headwinds, remembering that I'll need to return to my point of origin. I seek a return route that is sheltered from the wind, but the wind may change as I get to the shore that should be sheltered. I suspect some of that wind direction change is due to eddies, swirling edge patterns that occur along the wall of tall trees on the shore. Those trees create the basin, and the wind curls back on itself near the shorelines. So far, I've never had to give up, put the boat on shore, and walk back home into the wind. It may happen on Long Pond on some future windy day. I hope not.

We think of the wind as a horizontal force, but on gusty days it sometimes pounds down on the lake surface vertically. The impact spreads circular waves, then dissipates and does not push on across the lake as the impact of horizontal wind and waves does. The prevailing horizontal winds from the west often push up small ripple waves in a fingerprint pattern, in a pattern probably as unique as our human fingerprints. Watching those ripples disperse and be replaced is fascinating. Not so much fun when paddling into the wind, but still entertaining. As the wind velocity picks up, the waves enlarge into rolling breakers, which can have foamy whitecaps at the crest, which is a clear sign to promptly end a canoe excursion, even in warm weather and water.

We live only a few hundred yards south of State Route 28, the commercial avenue of the southern half of the Cape. It begins east of the Cape and transits the west and south shores, with stoplights every mile or two. Most of it is two lanes, as is the stretch near us, but some busy stretches have been widened to four lanes. Often the wind will carry tire noise or a passing ambulance siren into earshot of us across the lake. My peace during a paddle excursion may also be interrupted by a leaf blower, lawn mower, or the back-up beeper of a construction vehicle. Those noises intrude briefly, but I bring my thoughts back to the moment, the lake conditions, the pull of the paddle, and the direction of travel of the boat. The external noises interrupt but do not stop my paddling tranquility. Sigurd Olsen writes of the same annoyance, hearing a far-off train whistle from his "listening point," a retreat spot he purchased on a remote lake near the Minnesota-Canada border. After consideration, he realized the whistle represented progress, which also brought benefit to him, so he accepted it without further irritation. I have likewise been able to rationalize the car or ambulance noise on my lake and to let it go and move on. Daniel Boone claimed that visible smoke from a neighbor's cabin was sufficient incentive for him to move his family farther west, away from civilization. Later, the government proclaimed that the frontier was closed in 1888. I can accept that conclusion, and will not let road noise motivate me to find a more remote home.

Aristotle used the term *koinoi topoi* to mean "commonplace," an experience that was familiar without explanation to his audience, both in frequency and in understanding. In that spirit, I have become intimate with the details of this kettle pond. It covers only fifty acres, about one thousand meters in its longest dimension. I notice when winds change, or the transient mergansers or ospreys arrive, or a small tree has blown down in the recent storm, or a dock is back in the water after being stored on land all winter. I enjoy that *koinoi topoi* familiarity with my pond.

The canoe is an ideal instrument for gliding—peacefully, quietly, gently. I may interrupt paddling for a long silent glide to observe wildlife, or merely to savor the sensation of smooth, silent motion. In glide mode, I have encountered a turtle, basking on the surface on a warm summer day. He is alert, though, and dives before I can get too close to him. While cruising along the shore, I silently meditate. The Japanese might call those moments a *shinrin yoku*, meaning a "forest-bathing" stroll in the woods. Meditation is classically done while seated, but it can occur while moving—walking, paddling, or cycling. The key is staying "in the moment," not letting schedules, lists, or worldly issues (what the gurus call "monkey brain") intrude on the peace of that moment. Some walkers prefer a labyrinth for walking, to keep their minds empty of distractions. Paddling a quiet, open lake is the best meditation method I've ever used.

My canoe has no keel, so it tends to change direction (technically, to "yaw") with any slight wind or bump from a wave or the way I finish each paddle stroke. The continuous challenge of aiming the canoe can be annoying, but I read some wise advice from a veteran paddler, "A boat that tracks is a boat that's hard to turn." So on the flat and usually calm lake, I may be better off without a keel, to retain flexibility in direction and to stay in the moment.

I can move without any noise with careful handling of the paddle. It must be placed vertically and the blade buried before pulling. I prefer a straight paddle over one with a bent shaft, but not for any evidence-based reason. A clever lake guide wrote that the important difference between a bent-shaft paddle and a straight one is that one is bent. I raise the paddle out of the water without splashing to keep the silence going. I control the boat's direction with a J-stoke, but in a strong wind, I must switch the paddle from side to side to maintain forward momentum. This continuing challenge keeps me in the moment, mindful of the route I am seeking on the lake.

I prefer to paddle in the littoral, within fifty feet of the shore, where the water is shallow and the fish and lake bottom vegetation can be seen. The weeds and grasses cover most of the bottom of Long Pond, except in a few bare patches where the swans and geese have eaten. Several spots around the pond have broken tree branches or long planks of wood, likely washed out there from shore by a nor'easter in past years. Wood can last for decades or even centuries if immersed. A wooden ship in Sweden was brought up after three hundred years, gently preserved over twenty years, and is now on display there. The cellulose fibers, which fungi crave, are protected by another organic polymer, lignin, which water cannot dissolve. If no fungi or pests come along, as they do to wood lying on the ground, the wood can survive "waterlogged" for a long, long time. We see that longevity in evidence with the branches and planks on the shallow bottom of our pond.

We often have days that James Joyce termed "a day of dappled seaborne clouds." Fluffy white cumulus clouds with dark undersides drift by on gentle breezes. They remind me of the fine down feathers that the Canada geese leave on the water's surface during their molt. That down is a better insulator than any synthetic yet invented. The molt leaves them unable to fly for several weeks. They are often preoccupied with supervising goslings during their molt, so there is no inconvenience.

I usually see a lot of wildlife from the canoe. A green sunfish may be staking out his round nest in the bottom sand or guarding his offspring. A large snapping turtle appears on rare occasions, his head bigger than my fist, floating or walking along the bottom. Raccoons or muskrats, sly nocturnal scavengers, leave tracks on the beach sand. A great blue heron may be stalking stealthily along the shore, pecking up a small fish or another tasty morsel. Monarch butterflies flit from blossom to blossom on a robust buttonwood bush. Their habitat has been shrunk by the loss of natural flora and by fragmenting the shoreline forest into little Blenheim Palace lawns. The palace, with its fertilized, mown grass, is not a sustainable model to imitate with our lakeside yards.

I get great pleasure and relaxation from the canoe and paddling on the pond in amateur naturalist mode. My botany competence is quite amateur. I am a novice, but my intentions are good. I have formulated several rules for the twenty-first-century naturalist wannabe: First, patience. Viewing wildlife takes time, persistence, and effort. The ospreys show this trait. Keep trying. No hurry. The ten-minute observation periods required for herring counting can be tedious in a cold wind or drizzle. But rewards can occur at the very end of the period, such as a plethora of migrating herring or a beautiful birdcall.

Second, gentleness. Moving briskly among wildlife will usually frighten them, so slow motion without sound is best. No big arm swings or loud noises. Look far ahead to avoid close encounters that will frighten wildlife. Rendezvous with wildlife will be longer and more frequent if you don't disturb or scare them away. On Cape Cod, we don't have grizzly bears or rattlesnakes that we should intentionally alert to our presence with noisy motion.

Next, diversity. Observe a variety of environments to get the optimum nature experience. Change places, times of day, and weather conditions for your outings. Relish the awesome variety that nature can offer for your outdoor experiences.

Then, curiosity. There is too much to know about the natural world for one person to remember it all, even a professional. Fortunately, we have cell phones that connect to robust apps and endless Internet sources. They help identify birds and plants from the photos you take or the sounds they make, or show comparison photos to help with identity challenges. We don't need to gather items to remember our experience.

Aleksandr Solzhenitsyn wisely advised us to own only what can be easily carried and to let memories be the souvenirs of our travel. All you must do is bring your curiosity.

Finally, reverence. Treat each natural and living thing with compassion and courtesy. Assume every living thing is sentient and would feel pain from rough handling or being startled. Albert Schweitzer called it reverence for life, and it was the foundation of his inspiring and profound life philosophy. Take no souvenirs except photos, and leave only footprints as evidence of your passage.

There might be a better way than canoeing on Long Pond to be immersed in the moment, meditating as the canoe glides silently along, learning about the natural environment, and enjoying those fair winds and following seas. But I doubt it.

10

Paddling

The Value of Pure Quiet

~

canoe on the lake
glides silently with each stroke
moving meditation

Our lakeside cottage is charming and peaceful. On the rare occasions in my youth when I thought about being elderly and retired, I pictured living in an idyllic cabin like in the 1980s movie *On Golden Pond* or in the Quetico wilderness along the Minnesota-Canada border. Summers during my youth were filled with Boy Scout activities. There were many nights under a tent at scout camp, two multiweek hikes in the New Mexico mountains, and a memorable canoe trip along the Minnesota-Ontario border in the Boundary Waters wilderness with my dad, brother, and troop of scouts. I fell in love with lakes and canoes and learned the "J-stroke" on that trip. I am happy that such places still exist at this point in my life, and that mine is along the shore of a Cape Cod kettle pond. Our situation is better than any I imagined in those ancient reveries. Being lakeside every day is a dream come true.

The cottage where we live has an abundance of what Chinese cultural tradition would call "feng shui." The name means "wind-water." This practice reaches back five thousand years, emphasizing the impact of the surrounding nature on a structure, and the ways that wind, water, and nature enhance the flow of natural energy (*qi*, pronounced "chee") through the area. With the front of our cottage facing south for our solar panels and gardens, and the back facing the delightful water, our place on Long Pond would probably get a five-star feng shui rating.

The use of "nature prescriptions" in medicine is increasing. Encouraging a patient to get outside daily affects many aspects of physical and mental health. As a physician, I prescribe that for myself, following the advice "Heal thyself." The canoe is my usual partner in this endeavor. The six-foot grabber accompanies me on every paddling trip, so together we can keep Long Pond free of manmade objects and trash.

The beach where I launch the canoe is nearly level, so I have the challenge to get floating without getting wet feet or dragging the canoe across the sand and small rocks. After hundreds of launches and landings in the five years we have lived here, pushing the keel into the sand, most of the Kevlar coating has rubbed off down to the base layer on both ends. Now I don't drag or push it but lift it to move it. One of the wooden thwarts rotted and broke off. I bought a replacement thwart, and custom-cut it for the canoe. Back in business.

My canoe has only one seat, and I prefer to paddle alone. Jane often paddles with our Labrador, Rosie, held securely between her knees. Rosie did jump out once to defend Jane from a shoreline dog, but the water was shallow and not too cold. Since then, Rosie has been a reliable partner, watching the fish and sitting patiently on the centerline. For me, conversation and keeping close to a partner, canine or not, is a distraction from my goal of silent cruising. My favorite canoe guide–philosopher wrote that it is better to paddle solo and sleep tandem. I agree.

Once on the water, I guide the canoe with a quiet J-stroke and minimize splash and noise. One of my canoe technique books says that there is a proper way to twist the paddle at the end of the J-stroke to achieve optimal control and that doing it the opposite way is an uncivilized "goon stroke. " When I try it both ways (ending with palm up or with palm down), both seem equally facile and effective, so I suspect the book's opinion is hubris, not science.

Paddling silently is an art that requires continuous attention to detail. If the whole blade is gently and vertically immersed, there will be no splash or noise. The canoe may swivel and waves slap the bottom of the boat on a windy day, but with care that too can be avoided. The entire process is a "moving meditation," paddling silently, watching all around me and with minimum effort, breathing through my nose, and staying in the moment. The water's surface stillness can create a mirror of the sky, and an incoming osprey can be first detected by its reflection. I've attached a cushioned seat with an upright back to the canoe seat. It allows me to keep an erect posture. The practice is close to transcendental meditation. Zen paddling.

My working career was spent as an ophthalmologist and military officer, often in small rooms with the lights turned off. In those days, the weather had little impact on my life. Now, with a focus on canoeing, wildlife, and gardening, the weather has become an essential feature of life, especially when I paddle. On some days, I get into the canoe, expecting a tranquil experience, but the wind comes up, and the sky clouds over. The wind can change abruptly on a peninsula like Cape Cod, which sticks far out into the North Atlantic Ocean. I seek to paddle with little or no wind, but such a calm period is often a time of transition, when the wind is shifting in direction and the weather is changing. Depending on the speed with which the new weather is traveling, I may get caught in the wind after the transition. It pushes me around and raises waves that affect the canoe movement. I try to not let the weather ruin the trip. I may spot the monster snapper turtle at the northeast corner of the pond, floating or eating bottom vegetation in a shallow area. He disappears when the canoe passes by. He is at least twenty-four inches across his carapace, which is the maximum size listed in online descriptions.

When the spring morning is still, a mist may rise off the lake's surface, creating the image of King Arthur and the Lady of the Lake, to whom he gave his prized sword, Excalibur. A small lake in Cornwall claims that history. No Valkyries or ghosts have been observed in the mists on my pond, but I watch out for them. The mist is steam, moist air that has settled above the relatively warm surface of the lake mixed with colder air as it blows by, creating condensation. In October, the lake water is only 60 degrees, but colder air in the mornings is common. The autumn chill makes Long Pond so transparent and clear! I can see the pond vegetation twelve feet or more down. To paddle the canoe is enchanting. The fish and turtles have gone to sleep, so I don't see any of them. Our muskrat family left in the summer, and have not returned. Perhaps they found better hunting at Wequaquet or down at the salt marsh, and cannot return while the herring run is dry. I miss their companionship on the canoe excursions.

The waves come in a wide variety of sizes and shapes. My favorite condition for paddling is no waves at all—mirror-still. When that happens, moving in the canoe is an idyllic joy. If the wind builds, a gentle breeze may produce "fingerprint waves"—tiny closely spaced waves that move quickly but don't rock the canoe. Those waves remind me of the lines of a fingerprint. The breeze can add to the effort needed to complete the paddling trip, but it doesn't threaten to capsize the canoe or keep me from my planned route. Across the lake, those waves seem to disappear on the windward side, turning into a dull reflection of the opposite shoreline trees, then appearing as a smooth patch that is a mirage. If the wind picks up, the waves enlarge and become "rollers," wide taller waves that move fast. They push me around and affect at least half of my circular route around the periphery of the lake. Paddling against the headwind may be my only choice.

The most vigorous winds produce whitecaps, which we rarely see. Big or gusty winds, or when "small craft advisory" weather is inbound to Cape Cod, keep me and the canoe safely on our shore. On Jane's cousin's lake in Pennsylvania thirty years ago, I was paddling a two-person canoe alone against the wind, as the resonant Bob Seeger tune says, and making no progress. I had to come ashore and walk the last quarter mile back home. The canoe and I completed our paddling adventure the next day in calmer conditions. I have not suffered such a defeat on Long Pond.

Jane purchased a two-seat canoe with a cash graduation gift from her grandma in 1972. It is an attractive soft green fiberglass, in the size and shape of the Lockheed aluminum canoes we paddled in the Boundary Waters decades ago. Jane and I often took her boat out around Lake Wequaquet from Jane's parents' house with her cocker spaniel, Hildegarde. That boat, which we named for Hildey, traveled to California twice and must now have ten thousand miles of car roof travel on its resume. Recently, we made a return with it to Lake Wequaquet to find the herring run entrance. We found it after a long paddle west from our traditional launching site along the south shore. We were surprised to be able to enter the run and paddle to a tiny pond off the main lake. The herring run continues into a culvert under busy Phinneys Lane, where the wooden gate that controls the upper herring run flow rate is located. We could not approach that section due to multiflora rose thorns across the narrow width of the run. The natural resources officers who monitor the board gate and flow must walk to it from Phinneys Lane, as those multiflora roses rival the ones from Sleeping Beauty's castle. It was a memorable paddle, celebrating the fiftieth anniversary of many earlier trips on Lake Wequaquet in the same Hildey boat with the original, unforgettable Hildey.

My brother and I took an excursion around the pond in that canoe in 2021, remembering our paddling in the Boundary Waters fifty years earlier. A few months later, he died of COVID. His passing ended some of my connection with those great Minnesota lakes, and leaves a large gap in my life. We both served thirty years with the US Air Force but were very different animals. He was a fighter pilot and lifelong hunter. I never owned a gun, and get anxious if the commercial airliner banks more than 15 degrees. In high school, Jeff was a sprinter and long jumper, while my best event was the mile run. Yet we shared a love of canoeing and wilderness, with its precious and fragile nature. I miss him.

Alone, I have paddled that two-seat canoe by facing backward from the stern ("front") seat. The bow ("front end," although really it's the stern going first) raises several inches out of the water due to my weight, and waves slap on the bottom. The stern seat is closer to the middle of the canoe, so the elevation of the boat out of the water is less than if I sat in the bow seat. As Jane and I, and then Jeff and I, have shown, two passengers keep the entire canoe flat on the water. Either way, the bigger canoe has a keel and keeps its line better than the smaller, no-keel canoe.

Around the lake, most folks leave their kayaks, canoes, and stand-up paddleboards on or near their beach. Some leave their paddles in plain view nearby and not "secured." To my knowledge, there has never been a theft, although many other folks paddle by, and nonresidents can launch from the public way-to-water. Such honesty and convenience for all of us is wonderful. Sort of like being able to leave your home unlocked when you walk and not fear theft or intrusion.

When I am beneath a clear blue summer sky and a light breeze on a morning paddle, the usual cast of characters appears: goose, duck, osprey, heron, cormorant, muskrat, and turtle. Turtles are known for moving slowly, but they are also wary and stealthy, so I don't see them often. Often there are a few small floating patches of quillwort grass, then a pair of swans who may have been eating them. The swans and geese prefer to eat the pond weeds that surround the quillwort while leaving the thick, hollow quillwort stems floating. As they eat, they pay no attention to me, but the turtle disappears to the bottom when the canoe is several boat lengths away.

The mute swans, Canada geese, and several groups of small ducks—usually mallards and American black ducks—are present year-round. We see migratory mergansers and bufflehead ducks and a few loons for several weeks each spring and fall. An osprey or two may fly above, too timid to make a dive when I am near. A heron may flush from a nearby shore or tree before I even see him. The great blue heron is shy but one is usually silently stalking somewhere along the pond's shoreline. We also see green herons and black-crowned night herons, but they are seasonal, mostly when the herring are here. One cormorant will be on the lake throughout the year. They nest in colonies closer to salt water but come in daylight to feed here, usually alone. They are the most efficient of diving ducks, and their panache is on clear display in the middle of the pond. At the north herring run entrance, several large stationary bass guard the stream entrance during eel migration season. In springtime, I see half a dozen smaller fish, usually the green sunfish seeking a nesting site. It is idyllic. In the late summer afternoon, there is usually more balmy south wind and less wildlife to see.

Winter paddling, when there is no ice or wind, can be a fine experience. There are usually no other boats on the lake after November. I try to get out throughout the year, even when the water temperature drops below 50 degrees. I need mittens if the air temperature is below 45 degrees. January 2022 was an icy time and the first calendar month when I did not get out in the canoe at least once since we moved to Long Pond five years ago.

Years ago I competed in a springtime triathlon race, wearing a wetsuit for the one-mile cold-water swim. Halfway through the swim, I heard an unfamiliar honking sound. I stopped and looked for a nearby goose but saw none. After a few more strokes, I realized the noise was my own breathing. My vocal cords were spasming, as they had done in even colder water in the Grand Canyon when I was younger. I looked around for a rescue kayak, hoping that resting with my chest on its deck would allow my throat to relax and recover. There were no kayaks in sight. So I put my head back in the cold water and stroked on, hoping the spasm wouldn't increase. I survived that swim but don't want to repeat that horrifying experience in our cold-water lake. I am very cautious when the water is cold, except for one winter day in 2020 on Long Pond.

The lake was half ice, and both water and air temperatures were about 40 degrees. The water level was high and there was no breeze. The east lobe of the pond was mostly icebound, so I brashly struck out directly across the lake to the north herring run entrance, then turned west. I had to boldly break some thin ice along the shore, and was moving slowly and under control. I decided to pass beneath the arch of one of the fallen pines. There are three along there, and I've passed beneath all of them at least a hundred times, usually when the water level is lower. As I approached, one sharp broken branch loomed toward my head and the boat drift was taking me directly toward it. I raised my hand to slip around it, but I used the hand holding the paddle, which caught between the offending branch and another. Before I could react, I capsized and was underwater beneath the canoe. It happened so abruptly and unexpectedly that I am not sure exactly how I did it. I moved quickly to come up and thankfully could stand in knee-deep water. I don't think anyone saw the capsize, so the only rescuer was going to be me. I dragged the canoe to the closest shore, about twenty feet away, and flipped it to empty the cold water, which had filled it to the gunwales. I then quickly got in and paddled briskly back to the house, probably taking ten minutes or so. I was not shivering. As I was taking off my cold wet clothes on the back porch, Jane heard me and helped me to get into a warm shower. Chastised and more cautious in cold-water paddling now, I have confirmed that the fire department and the US Coast Guard are not close enough to save me from myself.

On some warmer days, I can complete a full lap around the lake. The wind or the rain or my bladder often limit the trips to half a circumference, either east or west. We live right in the middle, so each way is reasonable. One picture-perfect early spring day with a smooth pond, some adult herring and their delightful bow waves were visible along the north shore. At the north herring run entrance, one gull, two buffleheads, three mallards, and a couple of soaring ospreys were all present. The ducks could not swallow a twelve-inch herring, but the herring gull specializes in that particular fish. There were also some striped largemouth bass along the shore, awakened from their long winter's nap. Robins and red-winged blackbirds were chirping in the trees. A single cormorant cruised the middle of the pond, diving on occasion and catching a herring or another small fish. Further along, a muskrat carrying a mouthful of quillwort swam by. There were fragments all along that north shore—debris from his sloppy work. The muskrats eat the quillwort stems, but the geese and swans leave them floating, eating only the rootstock and surrounding pond weeds. I harvested a dozen or so floating pussy willow seedpods, and later put them under the leaves and wood chips along our shore. Jane has said she'd like to have more pussy willow trees on our property, so perhaps some of those seeds will grow. In addition to Jane, Rosie, and me, we have a lot of wildlife for one pond!

Early on a spring morning is usually an ideal time to paddle. The still water and the wildlife enchant me. Most of the waterfowl prefer to assemble in flocks, which seems safer to me. Both the cormorant and the occasional migrant loon are strictly solitary, except for their brief mating period. The mergansers and the cormorants are very shy, but the Canada geese don't mind me passing close by. The mergansers move on north by May. A muskrat may swim right past me. They dive when they see the canoe, but on occasion come back up near the canoe and start swimming on a collision course with its prow. Their forward view is sometimes blocked by a mouthful of quillwort, noses high in the air, headed for their nest. I suspect they are nearsighted, which is useful underwater but not so on the surface. In the spring, the naive muskrat pups venture out into the lake without adult supervision and allow the canoe to get between them and the nest. They then dive under my canoe and scurry back into a hole along the shore. One nest is near our property line with our next-door neighbor, and there are half a dozen other nest and den sites they maintain around the lake.

We have a close friend from college days who has a New Hampshire lake house. We paddle their kayaks on their much larger lake. We've seen a mother merganser and nine chicks sleeping at the end of their dock, while loons swim and dive nearby. Loons are known to need a long stretch to become airborne and can become trapped on small lakes, or if the water freezes and leaves only a small patch of open water. They hunt by sight, so cold water—which is clearer—suits them better. Their haunting cries enchant us at night. Truly a thin place, as the ancient Celts might say.

At Long Pond, many lake users my age are in pontoon motorboats. There are about a dozen around the pond, and most of them get out every week or two. Often the group conversation is loud, and their wake may be substantial, but otherwise they are relatively benign (compared, for example, to jet skis on Lake Wequaquet). Jane and I say that watching a big-screen video and turning on an electric fan would be the same experience. They are reminiscent of the giant inflatable rafts that we've seen on our two Grand Canyon raft trips. The big ones zoom by and complete the trip in three days. The riders sit up high and barely get wet, even in the big rapids. Our trip in three-person, oar-powered rafts took two weeks, and we got soaked in every rapid. A more authentic and memorable experience, in my humble opinion.

Paddling beneath a full moon during the warm water temperature months is a vivid exercise. During a "harvest" full moon with Mars nearby, I stepped out on the front porch to admire the big round glowing sphere and the *clair de lune* (moonlight) reflection on the water. The sky was clear, and the lake was mirror-smooth, indistinguishable from Golden Pond in the movie. A loon called repeatedly in its eerie, high, wailing trill. The feng shui was off the scale, and it was a lovely time to be outdoors after dark.

11
Canada Geese
Honking and Pooping

~

mirror lake marked
by V-wakes of Canada geese
feathered armada

We often have twenty Canada geese on our pond. On occasion, we have as many as fifty. When they cruise in low over the water, then land in formation, I am reminded of the Thunderbirds, the precision flying team in the US Air Force, with whom I served for over thirty years. The Canada geese are not as noisy as jet aircraft, but their loud calls do echo around the pond throughout the year. They are occasionally belligerent toward each other. They walk up onto the lakeside lawns to have a meal of the well-manicured grass. Then they poop all over the grass, leaving a mess that is easy to step in. Some of our neighbors have shoreline fences to keep the geese out. Of course, geese can fly and easily clear the low fences. We never have a goose poop problem on our shore, but we have some natural trees along the shore and don't have a lawn to attract the geese. I admit to some schadenfreude when there are geese on a neighbor's lawn. That's the same lawn whose fertilizer flows into our shared lake each summer, feeding the toxic algae bloom that closes the lake to swimming.

Canada geese live at Long Pond and Lake Wequaquet year-round. They were nearly extinct a century ago, but their numbers have skyrocketed since 1990, feeding on the vast lawns that humans have created and fertilized for them. Our resident geese are likely descendants of a captive-bred cohort, called "giant" geese, that was released by the federal government in the 1930s. The hope was to reverse the declining numbers of the iconic but overhunted geese. The descendants of that cohort do not choose to migrate but take up long-term residence in one place, like Long Pond. The Canada geese who do not have ancestors from the government release (called "lesser" geese) still migrate in beautiful V formations each fall. The two cohorts do not seem to interbreed, so they will probably evolve into two distinct species. The lesser migrators continue to struggle with hunting and predators, while the growing resident population of giants poops on our lawns without incoming gunfire all through the year—an unintended outcome of a wildlife management program. We humans fumble often when we try to modify the course of wildlife biology. With the gentrification of the pond's fishing cottages and larger lawns laid on our sand-covered rock, we will probably see members of both cohorts on Long Pond each year.

Last fall Jane heard one goose loudly protesting and saw that it was unable to fly. Later, twenty or so geese congregated in the water near the herring run. When they suddenly flew away, that one remained, this time showing an injured left wing. Jane called the town natural resources officers, whom we know well from their visits to oversee the sandbags and the herring run. One officer came soon and used my canoe to chase the injured bird. He was unable to catch it. It appeared to be wrapped in discarded fishing line, and when it was finally able to fly, it had a large white fishing lure in one foot. We hope the lure will fall out or allow the officer to get close enough to help it in the coming days. He said if the goose tires out, he may be able to catch it and remove the discarded fishing gear.

When the lake is frozen, we often see the geese walking on the ice. Recently two dozen Canada geese walked across the ice from the north herring run entrance to open water near our shore. Then they walked back. Awkward as their walk is, walking has been shown to use less of the geese's energy than flying. That makes their long migration flight efforts even more impressive.

In June, we may host a crew of six or more fluffy goslings, closely tailgating their mother. They grow quickly and by mid-month are half her size. By the time they reach that size, they will likely survive childhood. The Canada geese wisely use the warm weather of June and July for their annual feather molt, which prevents them from flying, but they are hovering over the goslings, so that is no problem.

The mallard chicks are much smaller and often come in larger groups. A substantial fraction of ducklings may not all share the same father. We hosted a mallard nest, hidden among Jane's garden abundance. Our Lab sniffed it and flushed the mother. No harm was done, and later we saw that eight eggs were present. She lays them one per day and leaves the nest unguarded between deposits. The embryos do not begin to develop until she sits on the nest, so they all are in synchrony, and hatch within hours of each other. Later, only two eggs remained. The mother can tell when eggs are not fertilized, and she rolls them away from the nest. Then the nest was empty, but we saw no ducklings. If the eggs hatch, the ducklings are precocious at birth, able to walk with their mother to the water within hours and to feed themselves without help. The tiny fluffballs blend into the vegetation along the shore very well with their mother. The royal green head and neck of the mallard fathers do not blend into the background nearly as well as their mates and progeny do, but they are usually nowhere to be seen when it is time for childcare. The snapping turtles hunt the ducklings diligently, with some success.

We have several mute swans on Long Pond intermittently. When there are three, one is often gray, likely a cygnet with its parents. We've never seen more than five. They are not native to North America, nor are they mute, but they have become quite comfortable here. The other two swan species in North America do not come to Cape Cod. The white feathers of our mute swans seem so unsullied and regal. They are stately and calm, even in wind and waves, and inspire us. Except when they reach deep into the water to eat and stick their tail feathers up to the sky. It reminds me of a college fraternity boy "mooning" the audience. Not dignified, but it does permit access to a lot more food on the bottom of the lake. The swans would likely tell me to look elsewhere if their behavior seems offensive to me. They can weigh fifty pounds, three times the weight of a large Canada goose, and can reach pond weeds at depths of five feet. They are rarely aggressive toward the geese, but on our pond, all seem to coexist side by side without conflict, that I have witnessed. When I paddle by, they don't pay any attention to me—truly unflappable.

CANADA GEESE

We frequently see a great blue heron, flying quietly on wide wings or silently stalking along the shore, hiding in the shadows, and then fiercely striking when she finds dinner. During the herring migration, we also see black-crowned night herons. They look like little old men in trench coats, crouching with their necks drawn in. As cunning hunters, they sit on overhanging branches, then pounce on herring or other prey in the water. Both herons have backward ankles halfway up their legs. They walk on their toes, so their ankles look like knees to us. They look so funny when they walk. They probably think the same about us. They are shy, and they flush way before I see them in the canoe, often flying to the far end of the pond to get away from the fearsome canoe and its occupant. Both these herons stay on Cape Cod all winter, with the great herons living year-round even up into Nova Scotia. Very hardy creatures. We've also had green herons, small birds that like both the overhanging branches and the shore. They stay while the herring adults are here, then migrate back to Florida for the winter.

Several times we've hosted a bald eagle at Long Pond. There has been a nesting pair on the Cape in recent years, after many decades without any nests. We've seen many eagles on visits to our daughter in Alaska (both bald and golden). Cape Cod is farther from Alaska than it is from England, so it's a real thrill to see one here. One cold day we saw one fly down the middle of the lake, swoop and grab a fish, then fly off. He did not jump in feetfirst as the osprey do. On another summer day, we saw an eagle having his fish lunch on the beach on the far shore. The red-winged blackbirds still had nestlings, and aggressively mobbed the eagle. The eagle took his fish and flew off. The use of DDT beat eagles and pelicans down, but both have largely recovered since we learned to use it more judiciously.

On the water, the diving ducks are the most entertaining. The buffleheads and mergansers arrive from the south when ice still covers parts of the lake. A dozen may be diving together in the middle of the lake. They are compact and round. They merely tip and vanish, without any bending or extending themselves or moving along the surface as they dive. They rarely stay down more than twenty seconds, nor transit too far from the spot where they enter their dive. The cormorant, a long, thin, pitch-black duck, dives much as a person would—a classic surface dive. They stretch out on the surface, bend in the middle, then disappear, their feet the last to go under. They stay down for a minute or more, often moving one hundred yards before they come back to the top. They are thought by scientists to be the most efficient underwater-swimming duck and virtuoso fishermen. Cormorants have a flexible lens in their eye that can bulge through the pupil and give them better underwater vision. Human lenses cannot bulge forward, but we don't chase fish underwater for a living. All the diving ducks are endlessly fun to watch when they permit it.

The pond hosts two species of cormorants, the double-crested and the great cormorant. Our cormorants are usually solitary, except briefly during mating season. Rarely there will be a second bird, not far away, in springtime. In September, we may see an adult bird with two smaller ones nearby— fledglings learning to fish. But most days we only see one. One clear, cool October morning we had a flock, called a "gulp," of sixty or so flying around. They did not cluster or form any Vs, but it was every bird for him- or herself, flying low and high, left and right, back and forth and in every direction, like bees near a beehive. Usually our solitary bird stays near the center of the pond, preferring to dive deep and keep away from the shore. He or she dives repeatedly, with little rest, and is very shy, often flying off when my canoe is one hundred yards away. Cormorant landings are ungainly, creating a big splash when they forget to land into the wind. They have short wings, designed to enhance their underwater skills, and are among the least efficient fliers in the bird world. When they take off, they gain altitude very slowly, usually having to circle around the pond to get high enough to clear the shoreline trees. They nest in colonies near the seashore, so our solitary fishermen are just on the pond for the hunting part of their day. When they swim, they sit very low in the water, barely showing any body, beak held up in the air in the distinctive profile of the most common grainy photos of the Loch Ness Monster. ("Nessie" would not like our shallow pond. Not deep enough for a sea serpent to escape the tour boats!) Some communities in Norway believed that those Vikings lost at sea could return to visit loved ones disguised as cormorants.

Cormorants need to dry their wings when they can. The double-crested ones are known for their wing-drying antics, with wings held out wide, reminding some of a crucifix. Occasionally, the cormorant sitting on a neighbor's dock in the midst of drying its outstretched wings will allow me to glide quietly by without flying off. They must be too warm and comfortable to scoot. One neighbor has a floating ball, about the size of a basketball, used for offshore boat docking. A single cormorant will use it for the wing-drying ritual, but staying on top as the floating ball rocks in the waves is a comical balancing act. It seems like resting on the stable flat dock would be a better choice.

The crafty gulls often soar and circle around our lake, then float in for a soft, gentle landing, like a ballerina on tippy toes. They lift off vertically, glide smoothly, and land gently. Their landings may be vertical, yet end in a gentle touchdown. They can nearly stop in midair, a few feet above the water. If they were delivering a full glass of water, none would spill. They seem to be the most efficient and adroit fliers of any of our birds at Long Pond, and would likely win any bird triathlon competition—swim, run, fly. They are good at all three. However, their social behavior is atrocious. They are scrappy scavengers, aggressive with each other, and voracious omnivores. We mostly see them during the herring migration in April and May, when they can capture a swimming lunch without much trouble. They hop from the surface and dive, with a high success rate, unlike the illustrious but often empty-footed ospreys. They soar and glide alone over the pond all twelve months of the year.

The mallards are our most common waterfowl, present year-round. Mallards don't poop in the public space as the Canada geese do. Ducks do not have an anal sphincter, so they poop spontaneously and surreptitiously, usually in the water. The geese perversely wait until they are on land, in spots where we soon will step.

Many mallards feed along our shore. They stick their heads down and raise their tails, just like the swans and geese do. That behavior is called dabbling, to distinguish it from diving to feed, which cormorants and mergansers do. Sometimes the mallards mate aggressively or chase each other. While watching for herring, I frequently have seen a pair of mallards zip down the herring run. They are very leery of me, even at a distance. They approach me on the herring counting perch and then withdraw several times, each time closer, then fly by rather than swim close to me.

Mallards have a distinctive landing, coming in fast then spreading their wings and tipping back into a "stall" attitude, as military aviators would say. The mallard landings remind me of navy jet landings on aircraft carriers. The pilot slows way down, puts the jet nose up to stall, then catches a big steel cable with a hook on the bottom of the jet. If he or she misses the hook, full power must be applied or the fifty-million-dollar plane and the pilot will quickly be in the ocean. Carrier pilots know exactly how many of those thrilling adventures they have survived, even when their count reaches several hundred. Each one mattered. The mallards risk much less with each landing and often make a big splash, but that doesn't bother them. If it did, they could watch the gulls and learn to touch down more gently. Or see one of the *Top Gun* movies for a landing lesson.

In my air force days, we would end our formal dinners with "carrier landings." The tables would be cleared, tablecloths removed, and beer splashed across the tabletop to lubricate the surface. Then inebriated pilots would take turns running and belly-landing across the beer-soaked table. Points were awarded for staying on the table. Quite memorable. As a physician for those pilots, I would stand by, and occasionally try a landing of my own. There were no casualties that could be acknowledged to higher headquarters.

12

Bird Life

Endless Activity

∼

watching birds is art
as they say, the more you look
the more you will see

The most recent common ancestor of both humans and birds was six hundred million years ago, before the "Cambrian explosion" of new life forms, and well before the dinosaurs ruled the earth. In fact, birds are living dinosaurs, with both the gull and pigeon thought to be descendants of Tyrannosaurus rex. Feathers were first seen on dinosaur fossils in 1996, and now scientists believe many dinosaurs were feathered. We share so little common heritage; zero shared changes in our DNA in 600 million years. While we like to attribute some bird traits to human behavior, and human traits to bird behavior, science would tell us otherwise. Nevertheless, both sets of animal behaviors are fascinating.

Much of what we know about North American bird life and appearance originates from the paintings and observations of John James Audubon. Audubon's practice of killing the birds that he painted two centuries ago has raised some concerns in recent years. Both Audubon's name and his names for birds could lose favor soon with the American Ornithological Society (AOS), the official bird naming organization, which is constantly changing the names of birds as new science or new cultural priorities occur. In a recent AOS decision, a former Confederate general lost his place in a bird species' name. Some bird names reflect a mood, such as those which name the colors of a bird during only the breeding season, while the bird has different colors the rest of the year. The "red-bellied woodpecker" has only a faint tinge of red on his belly. The "American black duck" often appears to be a gray-brown bird to me. Experienced birders know that Canada geese are not "Canadian" and gulls are not "seagulls." I know from past committee work that it is difficult to arrive at any decision, but some of the AOS bird names should be sent back to the committee for reconsideration.

Dozens of bird species populate our lakeside cottage grounds on Long Pond. While watching for upstream fish during a herring count period, I am surrounded by a diversity of bird songs, especially in the early morning. The revelry includes crows cawing, and a cooing of turtle doves can dominate the symphony, but the chorus of robins and red-winged blackbirds come through in the pauses. Blue jays squawk loudly too. Songbirds can be drowned out by the honking of Canada geese, the tap of a woodpecker, or the screech of a feeding gull. Ten different bird melodies may simultaneously resonate around me during my herring watch in the early morning. That symphony, greeting both the rising sun and potential mate birds, is one of the genuine joys of living near a Cape Cod kettle pond.

While many bird species migrate, Jane and I feed some of those who do not using two feeders hanging from wires attached to the back of the house and nearby oaks. We had them suspended from our deck railing but the squirrels would not leave them alone. Near the front windows is a cylinder feeder, designed to slip down and cover the openings when a squirrel hangs on it. The larger backyard feeder is a cylinder surrounded by a globe-shaped cage. Only the featherweight birds can get through the cage to the seeds without triggering the cover to close. The biggest bird to get inside the cage has been a downy woodpecker. The chickadees and nuthatches love it. The flickers and red-winged blackbirds can hang on to the lower wires of the cage and stick their long beaks into the cylinder, getting to the seeds. The squirrels are unable to raid it at all, although at a previous house they got frustrated and knocked it to the ground. Balancing on the suspending wire is hard for the squirrels, but they are very nimble and persistent.

Many songbirds now frequent our feeders, including chickadees, nuthatches, titmice, finches, sparrows, juncos, robins, blue jays, cardinals, flickers, nuthatches (both white- and red-breasted), and wrens. A few mallards stroll awkwardly up from the lake to scavenge under the feeders. The finches love to sit at the feeder and toss seed after seed to the ground, eating little, but the chickadees, titmice, and even the woodpecker will zip in, take one seed, then fly off to eat it on a nearby tree. They make a series of visits to the feeder and never stay more than a few seconds.

A definite feeder hierarchy is present. The chickadees, for example, are chased off the feeder by almost any other bird. Of all the chickadee species, we see only the black-capped one on Cape Cod. They take only one a single seed then fly to a safe place to eat it. They are masters of hiding seeds for winter then remembering where they are hidden, a marvelous and enviable skill. The titmice and the nuthatches are also small and easily scared off the feeder. We see both the larger white-breasted and tiny red-breasted nuthatch species at ours. They hop up the side of our oak trees, often facing downward and seeming to defy gravity. They must have very strong grasping toes to spend so much of their day on vertical tree bark surfaces. The little red-breasted version is low on the feeder pecking order, and—like the chickadees—takes only one seed and flies away. The nuthatches' less-common cousins, the brown creeper, usually only hop upward, and have a distinctive curved beak. Finches are not much bigger but punch above their weight, being less easily intimidated. They usually come as a group, pick through the feeder seeds, and stay on the feeder perch to eat until the much larger flicker arrives. The flicker is the apex bird at the feeder, a medium-sized woodpecker who can hang on to the cage wire for a long time, sticking his long beak into the cylinder feeder in the middle of the globe-shaped wire cage. He is not aggressive, but his size alone scares off the smaller birds. We have three other woodpeckers—the red-bellied, the hairy, and the downy—that visit our feeder on occasion. Blackbirds and blue jays hang on the outside of the globe cage but don't get much and can't hold on for long. Doves, cardinals, and robins don't try to come to the feeder but find dropped seeds on the ground beneath it. Robins are thought to be the most common bird in North America (other than the chicken) and seem to do just fine without our feeder.

Woodpeckers diverged in evolution from other birds nearly thirty million years ago. Of the over two hundred species of woodpecker worldwide, only sixteen are native to the Western Hemisphere, and only four reside on the Cape. Australia, New Guinea, New Zealand, and Madagascar have none at all. Each woodpecker species has its own unique tapping rhythm, which serves for identification, mating, calling, and finding insects for dinner.

We see only a third of the three dozen Western Hemisphere sparrow species on Cape Cod. Many stay in South America year-round. Others are limited to South Atlantic islands, as Darwin's famous finches are to the Galapagos Islands. Five sparrow species stay on Cape Cod all year, three more may be seen migrating through, three winter here from farther north, and five more come to breed but return south when the weather turns cool. To an amateur like me, they are all sparrows, but there are subtle differences in size, color, and habit that allow skilled observers to distinguish one from another. I keep a thumbnail sketch of the main features of all our resident species nearby when I am watching the activity on our feeders. So far, I've convinced myself that only two of those numerous species have taken our seeds. I'm sure I can improve my observation skills.

Wrens have a similar story. There are a dozen species in the Western Hemisphere, but we host only one year-round resident species, the Carolina wren. Three others pass through during the seasons. I can manage that level of complexity.

One of our shoreline oaks in our backyard has a fine deep round hole, about fifteen feet above the ground, directly facing our porch. We can see it easily from our living room and kitchen. It provides us with a bird's-eye view of many real-life dramas. Several years ago, an elegant flicker worked the edge of the hole, smoothing it like a fine carpenter. He then dove through into the cavity and spent hours in there, showing his head on occasion to flick out a beakful of wood chips. Many floated down on the canoe, which was stored on the ground beneath that tree. He must have spent a dozen hours or more over several days modifying the hole to his liking. Then a second flicker, presumably female, showed up and spent a lot of time inside also. We thought they might even have eggs in there. Suddenly we noticed a starling in the hole, and the flickers were gone. If there was a confrontation, we missed it. We don't know if the starling got the flicker eggs or merely bullied his or her way into the finely crafted nest site. Either way, we were deeply disappointed. We did not see baby or fledgling starlings either.

The following year a couple of flickers again cleaned out the hole, then took turns sitting inside, as if there were eggs. One morning one flicker was in the hole when a squirrel came up the tree. The flicker came out and went after him, pecking and swirling, but the squirrel dove into the hole. He was only in there for two seconds, but he must have destroyed the eggs. Half an hour later, the two flickers sat side-by-side, about a foot below the hole. They seemed to be very solemn. One would suddenly throw back her head and sing and the other quickly joined in, and they sang together for a few seconds. Then another minute of solemn silence. This shared singing routine recurred about six times. A third flicker was fifteen feet away on another oak, respectfully and quietly being supportive, like a pastor or family friend. Suddenly all three flew briskly away across the pond, not looking back. It may have been a funeral ritual for the lost eggs.

Two weeks later, that couple or two other flickers were back, cleaning debris from the hole and sitting in it for long periods of time. A few days after that we saw a homely starling carry a mouthful of grass into the hole. The family of flickers had again been evicted, just like last year. We took down our birdfeeders, but the starlings stayed. In mid-June, the nasty squirrel invaded the hole and presumably killed the starling nestlings. That squirrel or a cousin was stuffing oak leaves and twigs into the hole in September, making it ready for his winter's nap. The drama has no end.

The only hummingbird to come to Cape Cod is the ruby-throated species. One year we saw one set up her nest within view of our porch, using a pitch pine branch about twenty feet above the ground. It was exposed and easy to see from our porch, nestled into the elbow of a dead branch. Soon we could see two small beaks poking upward whenever the mother bird returned. Abruptly one morning the nest was gone. Later I found it on the ground, without evidence of any baby birds or even an eggshell. Living in the natural world is harsh and unforgiving.

We have raptors, including the Cooper's hawk, which specializes in taking songbirds at feeders. I've seen only one fly by our feeders once. The hummingbird nest destroyer was likely

OSPREY

a starling, blue jay, or squirrel. We see those much more often, and they are large enough to do that damage without remorse.

We usually host summertime ospreys, sometimes two or three at once, soaring and diving. They perch on horizontal dead upper oak branches that extend out over our shore, or at the top of a pine. A group of osprey is a duet, not a flock. They are wise enough to molt their feathers gradually throughout the year so the molt does not affect their fish hunting or delay their departure in late September. They never dive for a fish near the canoe, even though they often glide gracefully overhead. They may soar one hundred feet above the water's surface, which seems too high to be prepared for a quick pounce on a fish. They have sharp vision and must need the altitude to scan more water surface area, or to properly accelerate toward their prey.

Ospreys are persistent fishermen. They dive fast and hard, feet first, and hit the water with a noisy, powerful impact. They may drop what they do catch, and their success rate is only 10 percent. When they do get a fish, they retire to the top of a shoreline tree, where I have inadvertently flushed them in the middle of a meal. A silent canoe, moving slowly along the shore, would not seem like a threat to a feeding raptor perched high in a tree, but somehow it is. If the osprey is visible, I detour widely around its tree perch. They use our oak trees for scanning, hunting, and eating, and have dropped scraps of fish into the water near our herring run. They tear up their food, one bite at a time, so dropping a chunk is easy to do. They wisely migrate south in the autumn when the fish in the pond go deep to sleep.

The incredible capacities of raptor super vision demonstrate the limitations of our human perception. Many birds and bees see wavelengths in the infrared and ultraviolet spectrum, beyond human capabilities. Like Superman with his famous X-ray vision! Plus most birds have 360-degree peripheral vision due to the placement of their eyes on the head and the fact that they don't have prominent eyebrows.

We have frequently seen a great blue heron near our herring run, and one is on the lake almost every day. He steps with grace, neck coiled and sharp beak pointed down at potential prey. When he moves, he is an elegant flier. His large wings flap slowly and majestically as he moves to new hunting grounds, feet extended straight back, like a spear flying slowly through the air. If he calls as he flies, anyone nearby is certain they are witnessing an ancient pterodactyl.

On occasion, we host an egret, either a migrant great egret or one of our year-round snowy ones. They are much like the heron in habits, and stunningly beautiful birds. None of the cranes of North America appears on Cape Cod.

We have hosted a single sanderling, working the edge of Long Pond as he would the ocean beach. Perhaps he was blown here by strong winds and could not find his way back to salt water. He uses his sensitive beak tip and tongue to sense small animals within the sand. Within a few days, he is gone. Occasionally a single kingfisher, often with a small fish in his beak, will appear along our lake. These are known to nest in sandy banks above the water, and there are no such habitats along the shores of our pond. The kingfisher must be able to burrow into the bank, and it must be too steep for predators to climb. Appropriate nesting habitat is rare enough that many scientists believe it may be the limiting factor in the kingfisher population. I don't know of such habitat near us, but we still see them on occasion.

The red-tailed hawks are our year-round raptors. Their plumage varies widely from bird to bird, but their behavior and soaring flight are distinctive. They fly along the lake shore and perch on the tops of the pine trees, much as the ospreys do in the warm months. There are plenty of chipmunks and rabbits in our yard and around the pond, so these hawks do well. The chipmunks climb briskly up our oaks and maples, leaving their familiar horizontal world and exposing themselves to an aerial predator. I have only once seen an owl near our pond, a snowy owl flying from one shore to another at midday on a cloudy day. We have at least five owl species that nest on Cape Cod, and three more that come through intermittently. They are usually invisible to me.

We have seen Baltimore orioles many times. Jane saw them in the front yard and put up our split-orange and grape jelly feeder, which they adore. They've been back to that feeder often. We saw a nest high in the trees last year, but this year we don't know where they nested. From their near-continuous presence at the orange and grape jelly feeder, they presumably are nearby. We saw a robin try to use that feeder, but his feet don't hold on to the thin perch tightly enough to get much. We put up a baffle last year to keep the squirrel away, and it seems to work well.

Scientists tell us that birds do not depend on feeders, and rarely get more than half of their nutrition there. They continue to forage as they normally would, whether a feeder is available or not. The main risks to bird health from feeders are contagious diseases, like finch conjunctivitis, or bacterial food contamination from not keeping the feeders clean.

A group of tree swallows sometimes roost on the dead oak branches about thirty feet above the lake on our shore, the same branches favored by the ospreys. The swallows swoop and dive to collect insects or zoom along a foot or two above the water's surface. There must be many bugs to feast on out there.

The cormorants seem to be the most timid of our birds, then the herons, who often flush long before I spot them along the shore, followed by the osprey. The ubiquitous mallards are cautious, but not shy. They become quite bold when the neighbors feed them, and they come to expect the same behavior from us. They will swim right up to the canoe or to us on our beach. The least shy are the Canada geese and mute swans, who pointedly ignore me, even at ten feet of separation.

The crows come by in a flock of ten or so. Such a group is called a "murder," an odd and ominous name. Perhaps Edgar Allen Poe chose it. The silly names for a group, bunch, or crowd of animals are a colorful feature of our language. The crows stop on high branches and look around before going after the feeder or seeds dropped on the ground. They flush easily if I move, even when I am indoors. None of the other feeder birds is so wary and alert.

The Audubon Great Marsh Wildlife Sanctuary on the Cape Cod Bay side of Barnstable, about five miles north of Long Pond, is a charming place for a short walk. More than a mile of trail in the woods borders the large salt marsh of Barnstable Harbor and Sandy Neck. The preserve is quiet and has several great lookout spots to see the harbor. I have walked there in midday with zero birds and not a song to be heard, other than a few gulls who cry from far off. Not like the many different bird songs at our cottage in the early morning. John James Audubon shot a lot of birds for his drawings, so perhaps he would not be surprised. The Audubon Society may have protected the area too late to save its birds.

13
Otters and Muskrats
Erratic Fellows

～

hop hop slide marks on
the lake ice from a traverse
of the otter last night

My younger brother was a lifelong hunter and a close observer of wildlife behavior. He majored in wildlife management in college, and I often told him that those two words do not belong in the same sentence. Together they are a non sequitur. He would smile and nod, sharing my insight. He did not trap muskrats or otters, but he knew a lot about their erratic behavior.

In geology, an erratic is a large stone, obviously out of place, left stranded far from its peers by glacial action. We find house-sized boulders alone in the woods on Cape Cod, scraped up, pushed for many miles, then abandoned by the retreat of the glaciers eighteen thousand years ago. On the geologic timescale, the boulder moved quickly. Both otters and muskrats remind me of such erratic behavior, as they migrate across, beneath, and on Long Pond. They can be out of their habitat, too.

In our first year living on the pond, we often saw river otters. They had two dens beneath shoreline trees with gnarly roots on the north shore, and we frequently saw their new pups. The adult otters are longer and more supple than the muskrats and are known to be more playful. The next year the otters disappeared and the muskrats moved in. Perhaps the otters found better hunting in the salt marsh or at Lake Wequaquet. They are certainly larger and nimble enough to evict the muskrats if they wanted to do so.

The year the otters left and the muskrats arrived, I thought perhaps we had misidentified the otters the previous year and had always been seeing muskrats. Or that I was misperceiving the muskrat arrivals and we were still hosting otters. Despite viewing videos and reading quite a lot, I remained ambivalent. Muskrats have rat tails (otter tails are wider at the base), no obvious long gray otter whiskers, and are short and plump, rather than long and sleek like otters. Muskrats swim flat on the surface, whereas otters keep their head up and their body submerged. Muskrats are rodents, like squirrels and beavers, while otters are in the weasel family. Eventually, I concluded there had been a transition and we did now have muskrats, after hosting river otters. Two pups and one adult muskrat (presumably the mother) occupied the same shoreline den where there were otters the previous summer.

In winter, the otters range widely looking for food. In winter we have seen a single hop-hop-hop-slide track, made at night across the snowy ice from our herring run to the north one, made as the otter traveled up to Lake Wequaquet. Once we saw a parallel track back the next day. Muskrats can hop but rarely slide or set out across the ice. Looking at my photo of the track on the ice, the natural resources officers from the town agreed the track was likely made by an otter.

The hop-hop-hop-slide pattern imitates the Morse code dot-dot-dot-dash, which was featured by the BBC as the "V for victory" sound during World War II. They used the opening notes of Beethoven's Fifth Symphony to signify Churchill's two-fingers-up victory sign. Of course, Beethoven was German! Keep calm and carry on. Here on Long Pond we needed some of that to get past the endless pandemic, and having evidence of an otter's scamper up to Lake Wequaquet helped us.

The delightful river otters can stay down for fifteen minutes when diving and can even work from a hole in the ice. In the Far North, they have been known to make an igloo over an ice hole. We don't have any of those, but we do have some other mysterious holes in our lake ice. None of the holes looks like it was cut with otter teeth. More likely, warm water from the aquifer, with bubbles rising to the surface, disturbed the thin ice as it solidified.

On a recent mild winter morning, we saw two otters diving off our shore into the mirror-calm lake. They are nearsighted, to help with their underwater hunting, so they may not have noticed us admiring them from shore. One came up with a large fish, who was probably somnolent in the cold water. Otters are omnivores but much prefer fish. They use their long cat whiskers to detect prey in the murky water, but probably did not need them in the clear winter water. We hope they were looking for a den to raise their pups this spring. They prefer to occupy existing dens rather than dig their own.

In the wee hours of a dark night during a springtime herring watch, I heard a large splash in the pond, as if our Labrador had jumped in. But she was next to me, so that wasn't what made the splashing noise. I shined the flashlight around but did not see the perpetrator. A week later, again counting herring in the wee hours of the morning, I saw a small cohort of herring swim up the run. Abruptly, a large otter burst into the herring run, snatched two herring in his mouth, and swam briskly down the run and out of sight. He must have been the noisy splasher from the earlier night. During a third encounter in the predawn hours, I heard him splash and slap the water but again did not see him. Good nighttime eating for otters when the herring are running. A neighbor down the herring run also saw a large otter, the size of a medium-sized dog, in daylight.

Since that first year, we've seen only muskrats, not otters, swimming in Long Pond. The muskrats often swim around the entrance to the herring run, and they have adopted the otter nests on the north shore of the lake. They also have four or five other nests, stacking up quillwort into offshore mounds that resemble small beaver lodges or using an otter den beneath the tangled roots of a shoreline tree. Their nests are disheveled piles of grass stems, usually beneath overhanging branches that touch the water. Their coming and going from the shoreline dens is obvious from their scratches in the sand near the submerged roots of a large tree along our neighbor's side of the herring run. A telltale sign. When the underwater sediment near the roots is not disturbed, no one is using that nest.

Muskrats are rodents and reproduce at prodigious rates. A family may have two or three litters of six to eight pups per year. They are fiercely territorial and will kill intruding muskrats who are not from their family. They swim with webbed hind feet and their scaly tail, which they use for propulsion and to guide their direction in the water. On land, they drag the tail in a characteristic fashion that can help to identify their tracks.

Muskrats are nocturnal, like most rodents, but daylight encounters are routine during my canoe expeditions. A muskrat may be swimming with a mouthful of quillwort, nose high, and unable to see around the load without turning its head. One I encountered was disheveled and small. Perhaps it was a yearling challenged by malnutrition or disease. A few hundred yards later, there was another, floating and also eating quillwort, not behaving so erratically.

The vivid evidence of the muskrats are the large piles of freshwater mollusk shells along the shore and into the herring run. There are hundreds of shiny shells in the shallow water.

MUSKRAT

The mother-of-pearl insides of the empty shells sparkle in the sunshine. In the winter, we've seen the muskrats pile up shells on the edge of the ice, about fifty feet offshore. A muskrat cannot open the shell while swimming, so it climbs up on the ice or the shore to eat. It quickly discards the empty shell nearby and is back in the water after another. The herring run and its entrance are literally coated with open mussel shells.

Linnaeus in 1758 described each of the half shells as a "valve," meaning the leaves of a door. Two valves hinged together to become a bivalve. Jane's dad was born in Bivalve, a tiny rural community on the eastern shore of Maryland, in serious salt-water mollusk harvesting country.

The muskrats left Long Pond in the late summer of 2022 when the herring runs were dry. Where they went or when they will return is a mystery. So as I write this, we have neither otters nor muskrats living at our pond, although we have seen a midwinter muskrat near the sandbags several times.

Days with light wind and smooth water expose the long, curved, hieroglyphic tracks of our freshwater mussels in the nearby sandy spots of the shallow water. The muskrats probably use the mollusk tracks as a neon arrow sign, pointing at the last sandy location where the mollusk buried itself. In terms of self-preservation, the freshwater mollusks should have designed a better way to get around, but they reproduce in such prodigious numbers that the species can survive despite its self-destructive behavior. They spawn once or twice each spring, when the water gets warm enough. The larvae then attach to a fish and ride around—not parasitic, just filter-feeding while attached, then drop off the fish and form a shell for adult life. Their elegant swirling marks in the sand remind me of delightful Arabic or Tibetan script—round, smooth, and artistic.

Our shoreline purple loosestrife was cut by the muskrat, but later the base of the stalks is still growing. The cut marks on the stalks are sharp with no crushing, so the muskrat teeth must be like scissors.

The wildlife of Long Pond is so complex and interconnected. River otters and muskrats demonstrate some of that connection to all of nature. Aldo Leopold, perhaps the first wildlife management professor in America, would have agreed. His years of predator control with the US Forest Service led him to realize how foolish such policies are. As soon as we begin to treat the deer population as a crop, to be nurtured by killing the wolves, we provoke an overpopulation crisis, wiping out the deer food and creating a famine among the deer. Leopold wrote that natural features are not commodities but an interwoven community, where each resident has its role and noneconomic value. When one piece of the ecosystem is pulled out like an erratic boulder, the system collapses. We see that often in wildlife management.

14
Fish and Turtles
Year-Round Swimmers

~

*eighteen-inch bass splash
marking a tail swish against
a nearby prey fish*

The water surface is an ecological niche known to scientists as the pleuston. It is a stark and unforgiving border in the natural world. Most creatures who live above it cannot survive beneath it for more than a few minutes. Most of those who are designed for life below the surface are not functional above it, except for a brief foray to snatch an insect. Cormorants, geese, swans, and other waterfowl thrive in both the surface and subsurface worlds. They dive or explore from their surface world into the murky subsurface depths, seeking pond weeds, fish, or eels. While their main existence is on or above the water surface, they visit and feed very effectively in the subsurface region that is so foreign to us. But they can quickly drown if they get caught underwater.

From a physics perspective, the water surface is an interface of dramatic contrasts. Water weighs eight hundred times more than air per unit volume, and has one hundred times its viscosity. When rain falls, each drop temporarily breaks the surrounding surface tension, and the canoe can move more easily (but getting wet is no fun). In a canoe on the water, one experiences both buoyance and surface tension, which combine to hold floating objects on the surface and impede the boat's forward progress. Water is also astonishing for its solvent properties, among the best for nonoily materials. Few fluids can match it.

Above the water's surface is another transparent fluid, flowing in winds and carrying pollen, chemical vapors, and life-giving oxygen. Birds use it as the medium to convey them from place to place. Viral particles in the pandemic floated in this fluid from person to person, killing millions. Smoke from my neighbor's lakeside campfire is carried over to our porch, or from my fire to his nose. Movement of the air fluid can create eddies along the tall trees of Long Pond's shoreline. The inhabitants of the air environment above the water surface are as diverse and fascinating as the water creatures below the surface.

Long Pond hosts its most effective summertime inhabitant of this surface barrier—water strider insects. Millions of these nimble six-legged fellows cover the lake's surface. Circular waves are created when they move. When the water is warm and placid, their small circular waves look like rain on the pond, although the sky is cloudless. They glide at spectacular speed, bouncing off each other in a saltatory style, covering over one hundred body lengths in a second. Zip and stop, zip and stop. They hibernate under leaves along the shore during cold weather, then return to the water and breed when the water gets to 72 degrees or warmer, which is usually early June on the pond. They are voracious predators of any bug floating on the surface, including their own kind. Their body and legs are covered in fine fur of air-trapping hair, which makes them unsinkable, even in big waves. They also spread their legs to distribute their weight over a wide area, which aids in flotation. They carry a scent gland on their thorax that is offensive to most fish, who ignore them. Their middle and back legs are used to guide and accelerate them toward prey or a breeding opportunity. The front legs are short, so their mouths are close to the insect food they capture on the lake's surface. They communicate with nearby striders by vibrating at different frequencies, which are transmitted by the water. High-frequency waves tell their neighbors of a threat or warning, while low-frequency vibrations are an invitation for mating. They ignore people and don't bite us as they come and go in the millions in several population surges on our lake each summer. Remarkable water surface inhabitants!

Turtles handle life both above and below the surface with great competence. During the herring migration, I noticed a snapping turtle, with a carapace twenty-four inches wide and a head the size of my fist, strolling along the bottom. The herring were giving him a wide berth as he walked out into the deeper water. On a previous spring day, a big snapping turtle laid several piles of eggs in Jane's compost and leaf piles. Our neighbors had 250 baby turtles in their suburban Boston backyard a few years earlier, but we did not see any baby turtles or shattered turtle eggs from our turtle. They may have hatched and escaped, but more likely a predator found the nest of eggs and may have also eaten the shells, as we did not

SNAPPING TURTLE

see any broken shells lying around. Nature can be brutal and harsh, "red in tooth and claw," as Tennyson wrote.

From the canoe on a warm day, I was able to sneak up within twenty feet behind a large turtle (carapace at least twenty inches in diameter) moving across the east lobe of the lake. He dove and disappeared when he saw me. Shortly afterward I came across two much smaller turtles (eight inches in diameter). Another time there were two, a hundred yards apart, floating lazily on the surface of the warm water at sunset. Once I approached our shore and saw two large snapping turtles belly to belly, rolling over and over in shallow water. They wrapped themselves around each other, biting at each other's necks. They flipped several times, making a lot of commotion. Then they released, and one left by an underwater route while the other floated on the surface for thirty feet or so. Perhaps that was his fist pump of victory. Neither seemed to be injured, but it was quite an epic battle, likely for territory and mating rights. I had seen these big guys a dozen times, but never near our shore. Despite this fighting episode, they are timid toward people in the water and known to be aggressive only if cornered on land.

I often see quillwort (*Isoetes* genus) on the pond surface. The quillwort makes up a small portion of the bottom vegetation, but it floats. There are six species of quillwort, two of which are endangered. A trained botanist can distinguish the species with a microscope. Ours is bright green with hollow leaves that all originate from the base of the stem, and reminds me of the leaves and roots of a garden onion. In some areas, all the vegetation was excavated off the bottom in path-like tracks about the width of a large turtle. These bare patches resemble areas that a large snapping turtle might have dug, seeking food hidden under the weeds and grass. There are also room-sized bare patches of lake bottom along the north shore. The swans may have pulled up the patches of bottom weeds, but the paths seem too deep for a swan or goose to have cleared it. There are even "bucket handle" tunnels in the turf, with two ends attached to the bottom on each side of the path but the other two long sides floating. I have never observed a turtle digging a path, nor can I find Internet confirmation of that behavior. I wrote to a faculty member at the University of Massachusetts who specializes in turtle behavior, and he was not familiar with that activity by turtles. The paths, tunnels, and bare patches in the deeper bottom vegetation may have been created by muskrats, with shallow water help from swans and geese. Turtles do not seem to be the perpetrators. I'll keep watching.

Hidden among the quillwort and pond weeds is the American eel. We occasionally see small black ones migrating into the lake with the alewife in the spring. They live their adult lives in the pond, then migrate to the Atlantic to spawn once and then die. Their progeny drift in the ocean for a year or more, then swim upstream to the home waters of their parents, to repopulate Long Pond and other fresh water in North America and Europe. When the large bass are waiting at the mouth of the herring run, they are likely hoping to snatch an incoming eel, as the herring are too large for them to swallow.

We have a variety of fish species in Long Pond. How did they arrive in an eighteen-thousand-year-old kettle pond that had no streams in or out until 1867? Were they introduced by Wampanoag fishermen or early European settlers? Even the river herring, annual visitors in vast numbers, return to their birthplace, so unless their ancestors got confused and took the wrong turn, they must have been introduced here as eggs or fry. We know from local history books that a fishing company for Lake Wequaquet was started in 1860. They may have brought in the first herring.

The fish of Long Pond face a variety of predators—larger fish, otters, muskrats, osprey, and fishermen. None of the fish is more vulnerable than the migrating river herring. The intrepid little fellows are bullied and preyed on by a host of hungry predators, who stalk the herring during both their entrance and exit migrations. In the small maple tree that extends out over the water at the entrance to our herring run, black-crowned night herons often perch with head down, peering intently at the water. Then one makes a quick jump down into the water and comes up with a meal. Osprey also catch their share in the daytime, and on multiple occasions, I have inadvertently flushed an osprey with his half-eaten dinner from the top of one of our shoreline oak trees.

In springtime, as the lake water warms, sunfish establish their nests in the sandy bottom of the shallow areas. The sunfish family includes both largemouth bass (our biggest fish) and smallmouth bass. The main occupants of the nests I see on the bottom are green sunfish, none more than eight inches in length. They have a prominent green spot behind their gills and a resplendent turquoise color to the tip of their tailfin. Most of the hundred-plus nests around the shallow parts of the lake are cleaned and occupied soon after the herring depart in late May. A few such nests are from smallmouth bass, but the green sunfish are much more common in our pond. The males begin to swirl and splash in a circular area of the bottom sand about three feet wide, cleaning it off for a nest, which they then occupy in May and June. The eggs hatch more quickly in sunny spots, so shallow warm water is best for the nest. Some nests are positioned close together, like cobblestones in a clump, but most are solitary. The feisty little guys aggressively zip out in defense when another fish passes within ten feet of their nest. They splash and chase briefly, then return to stand guard. They even confront my canoe, which seems heroic given our size asymmetry. Testosterone is a powerful hormone! If a passing female is impressed with the nest, she may lay her eggs there, and the male fertilizes them, then protects them until they hatch. After a few days to adjust, the father fish chases the fry away and abandons the nest, leaving a smooth clear circle on the lake bottom. His nest occupation may last six weeks in total. The eggs and fry are too small for me to recognize, so the nests always look bare. The nests can be out of synchrony with each other. Some of the guardian fish may be a consecutive occupant of the same nest, but a new potential father may dust off one of last year's nests rather than start fresh.

By late June, most of the nests are abandoned, and we see a lot of jumping and splashing in the middle of the pond, which is likely bass that are chasing the new fry. Occasionally a big bass will splash, stunning some of the tiny dark-skinned fish. The prey are bass or perch fry, as herring fry are silver, like their parents. We see those by the millions, mostly in schools in the shallow water along the shoreline. In our kayaks on the salt marsh, we have seen dozens of schools of two- to four-inch silver fry with forked tails, presumably river herring. We also saw several schools of larger oval white fish with prominent dorsal fins, which they projected above the water surface, like little sharks. Most likely perch.

Our pond still holds mysteries for me. As I learn more about life above and below the water's surface, new mysteries replace the ones I solve. But the surface remains a dramatic line of demarcation for most forms of life and will continue to garner our respect.

15

Salt Water

Exotic Habitat

～

warm sun and the sea
tide comes in and then goes out
salt marsh gets a flush

Half a mile down the herring run is the salt water of Nantucket Sound. We walk there at Craigville Beach often. Although only a mile as the crow flies, the weather, the tides, and the ecology there are strikingly different from those at Long Pond. The bird life we see along the salt marsh is different. More gulls, osprey nests on top of manmade poles, and occasionally brown pelicans. The white pelicans from the Gulf Coast do not stray this far north.

After eighteen thousand years of freshwater ecology, Long Pond might someday become salty from a variety of causes. Scientists believe that the ocean level has been two hundred feet above its present levels in past geological history. Sea level rise from climate change could come gradually on us, and perhaps sooner than we expect. The water level at the pond now is twenty-four to twenty-seven feet above the mean high tide level. The obstructions between us and the Nantucket Sound put our lake and home at low risk of damage from ocean storm surges. We have no history of such a vicious storm, and the great hurricanes of 1635, 1938, 1954, and 1991 were powerful and destructive. But there could someday be an enormous hurricane storm surge that would bring salt water to Long Pond.

Craigville Beach is a small sandbar on the south side of the larger Cape Cod sandbar. It is parallel to the coastline, resembling a narrow peninsula that is connected to the mainland on its east end. The long, wide beach faces south and is a protective barrier for its robust salt marsh. The salt marsh is the same shape, protected from most of the wave action. Its long thin topography affects the tides, which must travel rapidly to reach the distal end of the marsh before the tide change draws it back to the ocean. A large volume of seawater passes through the narrow channel to fulfill this tidal destiny. Often a brisk tidal current passes under the bridge that connects the beach to Centerville. Any salt marsh expeditions in small craft there must begin with timing dictated by the tide tables. We find a lot to explore.

The river herring, which arrive from the ocean each April and May, successfully make the transition from salt to fresh water and back again. They wait in the marsh until the water temperature in the freshwater herring run is just right before traveling up to Long Pond. Our river otters, former denizens of the pond, are likely living now in the salt marsh, only occasionally swimming up the herring run to feast on the pond's bounty. Our gulls, ospreys, and cormorants also make portions of their living in salt water. The transient diving ducks we see on our pond also do well in shallow saltwater environments as they migrate to their breeding grounds to the north. Only 20 percent of all bird species worldwide migrate, but those that do provide a true spectacle when they pass through Cape Cod each spring and fall.

As a seashore peninsula, Cape Cod experiences fog. Thoreau complained about the frequency of the fog in Truro, farther out the Cape toward the Atlantic. In 1856, during his fourth visit to Cape Cod, he wrote in his journal that a third of his days were foggy, and "you lose so many days by fog."[1] We get a ghostly mist on the pond's surface on autumn days when the water is warmer than the air. On other days, we get clouds on the ground, what we usually think of as fog, and likely what Thoreau was complaining about. These cloud fogs can be so dense that we cannot see the trees across the lake, two hundred yards away. Dense fogs also provide a welcome dampening of the vehicle sounds of State Route 28, not far from the north shore of Long Pond.

The climate on Cape Cod is dominated by the surrounding Atlantic Ocean, Nantucket Sound, and Cape Cod Bay waters. Having salt water all around produces inertia in the air temperature swings, which are slow to warm in the spring and then slow to cool in the fall. The ocean water is only 39 degrees Fahrenheit in early March, climbing slowly to about 70 degrees in August. The surrounding salt water keeps air temperatures cool until mid-May or later. So spring is slow to arrive. The predominant west wind of winter (interrupted by a few nor'easter storms) gradually yields to the pleasant southerly breezes in our extended summertime. We are lavishly compensated for the late arrival of spring by the mild summer temperatures, which rarely reach 90 degrees, and our prolonged, gentle autumn. Truly a mild four-season climate that is idyllic.

The idea of a warm spell after summertime is common in many cultures. The ancient Greeks called their autumn warm spell the "halcyon days," after a mythical story of a bird that could calm the ocean waves so it could make its nest on the water. A kingfisher genus carries the "halcyon" name, with a dozen species in southeast Asia and Africa. We have kingfishers, but none of the *Halcyon* genus on Cape Cod. Germans called their temperate autumn period the "Altweibersommer," or "old woman's summer." Many Eastern European languages use the same expression. Other European countries name the period after the feast day that happens at the same time. In the southern countries of South America, mild autumn days are known as "little summer," *veranito*. Any nice name for those serene, sunny autumn days seems fine to me. A placid lake, clear sky, and 70-degree air are all one needs for a perfect canoe outing on the pond.

The spectacular volumes of pollution humankind has released into the atmosphere, mostly in my lifetime, will likely make halcyon days the new normal on Long Pond. We have known from Eunice Foote's work in 1856 that carbon dioxide is a greenhouse gas, trapping heat on the earth's surface like a feather comforter. The half-life of CO_2 is more than a century, but that tells us only when half of it will be recycled into vegetation. The second half will be half-gone in an additional century. The last 1 percent of extra CO_2 from current human emissions will not be removed from the sky for a millennium. Methane, euphemistically called "natural gas," is a more potent greenhouse gas but takes only a decade for half of it to leave the atmosphere. We've had two gas pipe leaks on our street in the five years we've lived on Long Pond, so you know lots of unburned methane is escaping to the sky daily. There are many encouraging technologies to "mitigate" and remove these harmful pollutants from the sky, and the sooner we implement them, the better for all of us and our bird, animal, and plant friends. Extending our mild autumn days through February will make life difficult or impossible for many of them.

Jane and I enjoy the salt marsh in our kayaks. We use the tides to our advantage and usually pick a calm weekday with no motorboat traffic. One summer day we launched our kayaks from Dowses Beach in Osterville just before high tide. The tides on this day were not as high as they would be during the full moon. The weather was quiet, with no wind and light overcast skies. We paddled west along the salt marsh behind Craigville's Long Beach, then turned up the Bumps River under the Main Street bridge. About a mile up the river, we came to the wide Scudder Bay and made a lap around it. By now, we were past the high tide and hoping for an ebb tide ride back to the beach. My guidebook says it takes over two hours for the high tide to turn at the top of Scudder Bay, but we didn't need it. When we were back under the Main Street bridge, there was a gentle onshore breeze, and it was difficult to tell if there was any inflow or outflow. We arrived back at Dowses Beach having seen only one moving motorboat. The guidebook recommended not doing this route in summer due to motorboat traffic. I was anxious about riding big wake waves in my kayak, and some of the tied-up motorboats we paddled past had two three-hundred-horsepower or four two-hundred-horsepower engines. We saw several sets of jet skis, but none were in operation. All in all, a perfect outing.

Another day we paddled on the salt marsh to the bottom of our Centerville River herring run, where the water is choked with an invasive weed called phragmites, a dense marsh grass like the Nile bulrushes that hid the infant Moses several thousand years ago. The weed likely arrived here in ship ballast from Europe in the 1800s. Jane and I maneuvered our kayaks through the dense growth to reach the bottom of the run. Access is not completely choked off, but getting there is a lot of work. I hope it will not deter the migrating herring.

Centerville's other herring stream, which comes out from Red Lilly Pond near Craigville, is quite shallow and also choked with phragmites. That lake is only a few feet above sea level, so the flow out is slow and gentle. The town natural resources department has said that phragmites invasion is worse for that herring run, but from a kayak view along the salt marsh, ours looks worse. Phragmites can be cut back annually, and after five years may sometimes give up. It may someday make its way up our herring run to Long Pond. The local natural resources officers are on alert for it each year, as they clear other wintertime brush to give the herring a safe route. The ospreys, gulls, and pelicans appreciate it, just as they will if we can slow climate change.

16

Trash and Externalities

The Long View

~

many eons from now
how will our remains be viewed
tiny bits of plastic

On my daily paddle excursions around Long Pond, I carry a grabber, a six-foot-long cane essential for snatching inappropriate items from the bottom of the lake and putting them where they belong—in the recycling or trash bin. The top priority is removing the plastic "forever" trash, which is unsightly and would never degrade to become a part of the natural ecosystem.

In my Boy Scout days, I tried to follow the institutional guidance to do a good turn daily. Picking up loose trash would meet that requirement. That habit has carried over into my current behavior. Adults should clean up their own messes. Future generations should not have to clean up the messes we make. Not fair.

I remember swimming in one of the pristine lakes in the Boundary Waters wilderness in Canada in 1971. We were at least fifty miles from any road. Diving down ten feet or more below the surface, I encountered a sunken metal five-gallon gas can. I was heartbroken to find human trash in such a remote, primitive place. In hindsight, plastic trash would have been even more discouraging, but it was fortunately rare in those days. At least that gas container will soon rust and return to the earth.

John Muir's powerful words on the interdependence of all living things touch me. "When we try to pick out anything by itself, we find it hitched to everything else in the universe."[1] Killing predators affects prey numbers and then food availability. Adding pollutants or trash to the pond affects the fish, the raptors, the river otters, and the humans who use the lake. It's not merely a simple act but a cascade of events that affect many more sentient beings.

In my youth, most roadside trash consisted of beer cans, candy wrappers, and cigarette butts. Now it is mostly seventy-five-cubic-centimeter plastic "nip" bottles. I fear for the competence of the car occupants who have consumed those bottles, and the innocents who share the road with them. On the lake bottom here in recent years, I have retrieved a fair number of old beer bottles and cans, but often now I find plastic water bottles. On my first paddling trips on the pond, I often saw long white earthworm-shaped items on the lake bottom. The first one I retrieved appeared to be an egg case of an unknown aquatic resident, so I put it back. After seeing others, I brought one home for dissection. An Internet search revealed its purpose—a plastic bass lure. That knowledge freed me to retrieve the rest of those unsightly items off the lake bottom without depriving any poor animal of its opportunity to propagate. Just trash from a careless fisherman. There are many of them, so they must not attach to the fishhooks very effectively. They are plastic, so they would never biodegrade into natural materials.

Another lake user thought it was amusing to scatter golf balls around the pond. I have picked up dozens from around the shoreline. They were likely driven or thrown from a passing pontoon boat, the perpetrator forgetting that the bright white debris would mark the bottom for decades. A bright white golf ball is not part of the natural environment, and that offends me. So out they come, and I go off to the public landfill with my garbage. I prefer Long Pond in its natural state.

The lake has two public ways-to-water, access sites for any visitor to reach the water to fish or swim. On the west end of the pond, a sloping road provides access for boat trailers to enter. At the east end, a small crescent-shaped beach has buried wood posts to block vehicles and boat trailers, but with parking and a sandy beach. The spot is relatively secluded, not near other houses. Portable fishing boats are often launched from the back of pickup trucks there. Swimmers and shoreline fishermen use this spot. Weekend drinking parties sometimes also take place there. Like teenagers everywhere (including me at that age), the kids leave their beer cans and bottles. We did not have the plastic "nip" bottles in my youth, and now those awful containers make up much of the debris. When the trash buildup is too great, I land my canoe and pick up as much of the visible trash as I can. Often I nearly fill the front of the canoe with cans and plastic bottles. A better town government would provide trash and recycling containers for their public beach, and empty them periodically. I have written the town requesting trash service there. But if they won't do it, I will.

One sparkling summer day I retrieved an old beer bottle from the mud on the bottom of a still section of the pond. I placed it in the bow of the canoe with other trash items. A few minutes later, a squirming one-foot black eel startled me, wiggling vigorously in a shallow puddle near the trash. I must have disturbed his habitat by removing his home. Feeling guilty, I placed him gently back into the water, hoping he would find a safe place on the bottom before a predator found him. He or she survived the dangerous catadromous migration, the heroic return to fresh water to live most of his adult life after birth in the middle of the ocean. I wish I understood more of the factors that make that choice wise and sustainable. An epic trip for a small, vulnerable creature. I want to respect that accomplishment. But he needs to find a natural home. Sorry.

While trash seems to be everywhere, we have reasons for optimism. Our species can learn and change. We beat the ozone-layer-depleting chemicals in the 1980s by changing policy and behavior. The whooping cranes numbered only twenty in the United States in 1961 but now have recovered to over six hundred. There were only 350 bison left in 1883, but today we have 200,000. The river otter population in my home state of Missouri was down to seventy when my dad was a boy in the 1930s, but today there are ten thousand. We've recovered from environmental folly repeatedly, and can do it again with our single-use plastic debris.

An externality is defined as the transaction cost to an uninvolved third party. One guy buys a "nip" bottle to consume some alcohol, and the liquor company makes a profit, but the rest of us suffer from the roadside trash externality and gain nothing. The trash in the lake fits that description. An effective government would create better incentives and rules to minimize externalities. The town of Barnstable hopes that by not providing a trash can and pickup service at its public way-to-water, people will take their own trash home. What an imaginary world! I think it is just an excuse for not using taxpayers' funds to do a government task. Trash is everyone's problem, and public funds should be used to minimize it.

Change over the centuries reminds me of an article for a medical journal I wrote a few years ago titled "The 21st Century

Trajectory of Global Health."[2] I proposed that the trajectory of progress in global health is a sigmoid curve, one that resembles a capital *S* leaning forward. Initially progress is slow, then accelerates upward, reaches an exponential upslope, then the trajectory of progress slows at a high plateau level. I suggested we are in the slow buildup phase of global health progress now, but approaching a dramatic upslope soon. Eventually, new knowledge and teamwork accumulate into a critical mass and we will reach a plateau of worldwide good health for humans and other living beings. It is an optimistic perspective. I think history will show that trajectory is correct.

Many natural and human functions are sigmoid. We have an economic and a social/cultural/political trajectory, both of which have superimposed small cycles with the major trend relentlessly upward. We are near the nadir in a short cycle now, with polarization and great inequality, and reactionaries pulling us backward. I predict the cycle will soon shift back to robust social and economic progress. Another trajectory is technological, and it too is sigmoid and relentlessly upward. We may have been on the steep upward section of the technology trajectory since the Renaissance, with a Moore's law spurt in my lifetime. Will there be a "top-of-the-S" plateau someday? I don't see it yet.

Trends and trajectories are part of taking the long view, a topic I used in a medical school commencement speech a decade ago. One can be discouraged by temporary roadblocks or idiotic reactionary behavior, as with congressional gridlock. We seemed to have the environmental movement on a fast upward trajectory fifty years ago. "Biodegradable" was a worthy attribute for a product and its packaging, and worth paying for. No longer. But when we think with a long view about the progress in one hundred or one thousand years, it is clear that we have made great progress. Such long views are not part of traditional thinking or our news reporting, but they should be. They show us reality, the long view trajectory of progress.

The natural history of Cape Cod illustrates the importance of taking a long view of our environment. On its eastern shore along the Atlantic Ocean coast, erosion is measured in feet per year, squeezing that narrow land into a thinner and thinner peninsula. Houses drop off the tall sand cliffs with regularity, as the storms undercut them. Climate change may accelerate that process. Our time to relish those sandy gems is limited, even though we are fortunate that so much of it is protected by "National Seashore" status. Long Pond and the rest of the Cape seem less fragile and threatened, but also have limited capacity for human neglect and abuse. Single-use plastic trash, PFAS, algae blooms, atmospheric pollutants, and other human debris accumulate quickly on a geological timescale. We must take a long view toward reducing these threats to the Cape environment.

As Aldo Leopold wisely advised us, reducing our long-term impact, supporting the natural processes and native species, living sustainably on a piece of land—those are challenging and noble goals. We understand how connected all of nature, including Homo sapiens, are to each other, and the wisdom of Leopold's insight should predominate in our public policy and private actions.

Leopold was a fisherman, a hunter, and a careful observer of nature. His writings on conservation and environmental ethics were tempered by his enjoyment of killing animals and fish. He wrote of sportsmanship, and he both respected and sought to understand his prey. He wrote of the importance of a balance between predator and prey in nature. And he wrote eloquently about a "land ethic" many decades before the larger environmental movement caught up with his thoughts.

He was a cigarette smoker, and I have wondered how he disposed of his cigarette butts. He may not have used them, since cigarette filters were not introduced until the 1930s and rarely sold until after World War II. Leopold died in 1948 of a heart attack, the most common cause of death in smokers. Today cigarette filters are the most common item of trash in our oceans worldwide. In the air force, basic trainees who smoke are forbidden by their drill sergeant from discarding their cigarette butts on the ground. After they smoke, they must extinguish their cigarette, break off the remaining tobacco part, then put the bare filter into their pocket for later disposal in a trash can. Perhaps Leopold did that, too, or never smoked a filtered cigarette. He was an inspiring visionary that we lost too soon.

Another clever philosophical insight into environmental ethics comes from the eminent humanitarian Albert Schweitzer. He writes of struggling to assemble a coherent philosophy for his life after leaving a career in Europe as a world-class organist and theology scholar. He chose to work as a missionary physician in the West African jungle. While there, he was traveling on a slow boat to make a house call on a patient when he had his insight—reverence for life.[3] He had dedicated his life to preserving other life, and reverence for life described this passion. He applied that concept to all living things, although he did not entirely give up animal meat in his diet.

Today we have much more evidence of the connections between all life—prey and predator, parasite and host, plant and animal. When one piece of the environment falls out, others suffer also. When there are few predators, the prey population explodes and eats all the available food, provoking a famine on its own kind. We must be wiser and more reverent toward all life in the future.

My recommended solution to the trash in Long Pond, the roadside, and the ocean can be summarized as non-zero-sum. Commercial transactions are zero-sum when one person loses as much as the other wins. If the transaction is structured so that both parties win, at least in part, the transaction becomes non-zero-sum. That is what happens with recycling. Both parties gain when the trash has value and we recycle it. The sum of the benefits is not zero but a net positive. With lifecycle responsibility, the manufacturer who makes a profit also takes responsibility for recycling the product and does not depend on public landfill, roadsides, or lake bottoms to collect it. We know how to do this, and must redouble our efforts to make the recycling of trash effective, natural, and ubiquitous. We can do this. The responsibility belongs to the manufacturers and to everyone. We can also shift from nonrecyclable materials such as single-use plastics to biodegradable materials that can be composted. Incentives by the government can be legislated to make this the default option for everyone, especially the manufacturers of single-use plastic. If they were responsible for disposing of and recycling their products, they would be enthusiastic about biodegradable packaging.

We have no reason for apathy or hopelessness in the face of the growing burden of plastic trash in Long Pond and in the environment. The same philosophy can create win-win synergies that slow climate change, social polarization, and economic inequalities. Synergies can put humankind on the steep upslope of the S curve to a sustainable, win-win future.

Robert Thorson wrote that lake management is people management.[4] Humans dominate the kettle pond ecology. We have not inherited the long Cape Cod moraine and its kettle ponds from our ancestors. We are borrowing them from our descendants. We can reduce our impact and restore the natural beauty and health of the Cape's environment for our grandchildren and their grandchildren so they do not need to carry a long trash grabber in their canoes in the future.

Notes

Preface

1. Sigurd F. Olsen, *Of Time and Place* (Saint Paul: University of Minnesota Press, 1982).
2. Henry David Thoreau, *Walden* (New York: Signet Books, 1949), 143.
3. *"The River of the Mother of God" and Other Essays by Aldo Leopold*, ed. J. Baird Callicott and Susan L. Flader (Madison: University of Wisconsin Press, 1991), 254. See also Aldo Leopold, *The Sand County Almanac* (New York: Oxford University Press, 1949).
4. Christopher Norwent, *North of Our Lives* (Camden, ME: Downeast Books, 1989); Christopher Norwent, *Return to Warden's Grove* (Iowa City: University of Iowa Press, 2007).
5. John Muir, *Travels in Alaska* (Boston: Mariner Books, 1879), 69.

1
Geology

1. Robert M. Thorson, *Beyond Walden* (New York: Walker, 2009), 1. Thorson takes the term from Robert Finch, *The Primal Place* (New York: W.W. Norton, 1983), 109.
2. Henry Beston, *The Outermost House* (New York: Ballantine, 1956).

3
Herring Run

1. Town of Barnstable, *The Seven Villages of Barnstable* (Barnstable, MA, 1976), 295.

2. Town of Barnstable, *Seven Villages of Barnstable*, 86.
3. John Hay, *The Run* (Boston: Beacon Press, 1959); Barbara Brennessel, *The Alewifes' Tale: The Life History and Ecology of River Herring in the Northeast* (Boston: University of Massachusetts Press, 2014).

4
Counting Herring

1. John Hay, *The Run* (Boston: Beacon Press, 1959), 135.

5
Springtime

1. Susan Simard, *Finding the Mother Tree: Discovering the Wisdom of the Forest* (New York: Alfred Knopf, 2021).

15
Salt Water

1. *The Writings of Henry David Thoreau: Journal*, ed. B. Torrey (Boston: Houghton-Mifflin, 1906), 448.

16
Trash and Externalities

1. John Muir, *My First Summer in the Sierra* (New York: Random House, 2003), 211.
2. Stephen G. Waller, "The 21st Century Trajectory of Global Health," *Annals of Global Health* 81, no. 5 (2015): 587, http://dx.doi.org/10.1016/j.aogh.2015.12.002.
3. Albert Schweitzer, *Out of My Life and Thought* (Baltimore: Hopkins Press, 1998), 155.
4. Robert M. Thorson, *Beyond Walden* (New York: Walker, 2009), 225.